Controlling Money

RALPH C. BRYANT

Controlling Money

The Federal Reserve and its Critics

THE BROOKINGS INSTITUTION
Washington, D.C.

1775 Massachusetts Avenue, N.W., Washington, D.C. 20036

Library of Congress Cataloging in Publication data:

Bryant, Ralph C., 1938–
Controlling money.
Includes bibliographical references and index.
1. Board of Governors of the Federal Reserve System (U.S.) 2. Monetary policy—United States. 3. Money supply—United States. I. Title.
HG2565.B79 1983 332.1'1'0973 82-45983
ISBN 0-8157-1136-0
ISBN 0-8157-1135-2 (pbk.)

9 8 7 6 5 4 3 2 1

THE BROOKINGS INSTITUTION is an independent organization devoted to nonpartisan research, education, and publication in economics, government, foreign policy, and the social sciences generally. Its principal purposes are to aid in the development of sound public policies and to promote public understanding of issues of national importance.

The Institution was founded on December 8, 1927, to merge the activities of the Institute for Government Research, founded in 1916, the Institute of Economics, founded in 1922, and the Robert Brookings Graduate School of Economics and Government, founded in 1924.

The Board of Trustees is responsible for the general administration of the Institution, while the immediate direction of the policies, program, and staff is vested in the President, assisted by an advisory committee of the officers and staff. The by-laws of the Institution state: "It is the function of the Trustees to make possible the conduct of scientific research, and publication, under the most favorable conditions, and to safeguard the independence of the research staff in the pursuit of their studies and in the publication of the results of such studies. It is not a part of their function to determine, control, or influence the conduct of particular investigations or the conclusions reached."

The President bears final responsibility for the decision to publish a manuscript as a Brookings book. In reaching his judgment on the competence, accuracy, and objectivity of each study, the President is advised by the director of the appropriate research program and weighs the views of a panel of expert outside readers who report to him in confidence on the quality of the work. Publication of a work signifies that it is deemed a competent treatment worthy of public consideration but does not imply endorsement of conclusions or recommendations.

The Institution maintains its position of neutrality on issues of public policy in order to safeguard the intellectual freedom of the staff. Hence interpretations or conclusions in Brookings publications should be understood to be solely those of the authors and should not be attributed to the Institution, to its trustees, officers, or other staff members, or to the organizations that support its research.

Foreword

For many decades economists have studied the channels through which the actions of a central bank influence the economy. Much attention has been devoted to the operating strategies of central banks and to the role that "money" should play in the formulation and implementation of policy decisions.

Controversy about these matters has a long history that continues to this day. Nonetheless, during the past decade a particular approach to monetary policy has gained broad acceptance in the United States and in many other industrial nations. That approach requires a nation's central bank to publicly announce a "target time path" for the national money stock (somehow defined) and then to use all its powers to make the actual stock follow that path closely. In essence, this strategy seeks to use money as a surrogate for the ultimate objectives of policy such as growth of real GNP, high employment, and low inflation.

Although many policymakers and economists endorse this approach for conducting Federal Reserve policy, it is open to serious objections on several grounds. Ralph C. Bryant summarizes these objections in this book. Bryant also discusses two common sources of confusion about Federal Reserve money targeting: an inadequate comprehension of the consequences of choosing among alternative operating strategies available to the Federal Reserve, and a tendency to ignore or de-emphasize the importance of nonpolicy factors in the determination of month-to-month variations in the money stock.

The conclusions developed here cannot accurately be categorized as either monetarist or antimonetarist. Thoughtful positions on the important issues about Federal Reserve policy do not lend themselves to such labels. A central purpose of the book is to put aside the sterile aspects of the long-standing debate between monetarists and Keynesians and to promote an informed discussion of the matters that genuinely deserve attention.

This book is an outgrowth of a manuscript originally prepared for a February 1982 conference on current issues in U.S. monetary policy sponsored by the American Enterprise Institute for Public Policy Research. An abridgement of the original paper was published in the *Journal of Money, Credit and Banking*, vol. 14 (November 1982), pt. 2, pp. 597–625.

Ralph C. Bryant, a senior fellow in the Brookings Economic Studies program, is also the author of *Money and Monetary Policy in Interdependent Nations* (Brookings, 1980) and of *Financial Interdependence and Variability in Exchange Rates* (Brookings, 1980). Before joining Brookings, he served on the staff of the Board of Governors of the Federal Reserve System as Director of the Division of International Finance and Associate Economist of the Federal Open Market Committee.

Several colleagues and friends helped the author during the course of his research and writing. In particular, he acknowledges the comments and assistance of Helen T. Farr, Bonnie Garrett, Dale W. Henderson, David E. Lindsey, Allan H. Meltzer, John Paulus, Richard D. Porter, Perry D. Quick, Paul Spindt, P.A.V.B. Swamy, and Peter A. Tinsley. Research assistance was provided by Eric Leeper, Christine Ross, and Arnold A. Sheetz and typing by Charlotte Kaiser. Karen J. Wirt edited the manuscript; the factual content was verified by Judith L. Cameron; and Florence Robinson prepared the index.

The views expressed here are those of the author and should not be ascribed to the trustees, officers, or other staff members of the Brookings Institution.

BRUCE K. MACLAURY
President

January 1983
Washington, D.C.

Contents

Appendix Tables

Text Figures

Appendix Figures

CHAPTER ONE

Introduction

It is widely believed that the money stock of the United States, somehow defined, should play a central role in the conduct of Federal Reserve monetary policy. In particular, it is believed that the Federal Reserve should publicly announce a target time path for the money stock and then try to make the actual stock follow that path closely. The analytical basis for this approach to monetary policy, however, is seriously deficient. Debate about the approach seldom focuses on the important, controversial issues about which views can justifiably differ; instead, the debate often becomes mired in confusion and spurious issues.

One source of confusion is an inadequate analysis of the operating procedures through which the Federal Reserve implements its policy from one short-run period to the next. In principle, the Federal Reserve can choose among several alternatives when selecting its operating procedures. The Federal Reserve did in fact change its operating procedures in October 1979. Both in theory and in practice the differences among alternative operating procedures and their implications for the money stock and for the economy tend to be poorly understood. Disagreement about the subject is rife, yet the participants in the controversy often fail to communicate effectively with each other.

Another source of confusion is a widespread misperception of the economic processes determining the money stock. Most noneconomists, and even many economists, seem to believe that the Federal Reserve can straightforwardly cause the money stock to follow a target path closely—month by month—provided only that the Federal Reserve conscientiously tries to do so. In fact, however, the *nonpolicy* factors helping to determine the month-to-month changes in the money stock are much more important than is generally understood.

A third source of confusion is a poor understanding of the two-stage decision process implicit in the strategy of using a target path for the money stock as a surrogate for the ultimate targets of economic policy.

In what follows I closely examine these three sources of confusion. My purpose is frankly pedagogical: to improve the level of understanding about the choices open to the Federal Reserve and the considerations that should influence those choices. I hope to foster a greater convergence of views where controversy derives from misunderstanding. When a convergence of views is not likely, I try to bring points of disagreement into clearer focus.

The international aspects of monetary policy are not discussed here. That omission is a serious shortcoming, and I feel very uncomfortable contributing to the tradition of discussing Federal Reserve policy as though the U.S. economy were closed to the rest of the world. The tendency to separate the domestic and external aspects of policy, like the separation of closed-economy theory and international economics from which it is derived, is a serious impediment to good policymaking. My omission of the external aspects is justified, if at all, only as a device to keep the exposition simpler and shorter.[1]

Chapter 2 provides an analytical description of how the money stock is influenced by nonpolicy factors under alternative Federal Reserve operating procedures. Chapter 3 comments on the implications of this analysis for the Federal Reserve's choice of operating procedure. The analysis in chapters 2 and 3 does not prejudice the issue of how closely the Federal Reserve should, or does, try to control the money stock. Chapters 4 through 6 focus on the ability of the Federal Reserve to control money in the short run (a period of two to three months or less). Chapter 7 discusses the control of the money stock over the medium and long run. The reasons why use of the money stock as a surrogate target is an inferior approach to the conduct of monetary policy are summarized in chapter 8. Chapter 9 discusses the extent to which the Federal Reserve has actually been pursuing the money-target approach and offers some observations on the least unsatisfactory way to implement the approach, given that the Federal Reserve and the Reagan administration are politically committed to it for the next year or two. The last chapter offers a comment on priorities for future research and debate.

1. My previous book emphasizes these aspects and indicates how they should be integrated with the analysis of domestic monetary policy. See Ralph C. Bryant, *Money and Monetary Policy in Interdependent Nations* (Brookings Institution, 1980).

CHAPTER TWO

Money Supply and Demand under Alternative Operating Procedures

A VARIETY of private financial intermediaries in the United States—commercial banks that are members of the Federal Reserve System, nonmember commercial banks, savings and loan associations, mutual savings banks, credit unions, and money market mutual funds—issue several types of deposit or deposit-like liabilities to firms and households. Some of these deposit liabilities are deemed to be "money." The others are more or less close substitutes for money. Because of this diversity, many alternative definitions of money can be, and have been, put forward. The situation is still more complex when analysis acknowledges the financial openness of the American economy (for example, holdings of liquid assets denominated in dollars and holdings by foreigners of liquid assets denominated in dollars and holdings by U.S. residents of liquid assets denominated in foreign currencies).

To grasp the most basic points about alternative operating procedures for the Federal Reserve and about the determination of the stock of money, however money may be defined, it is initially helpful to abstract from the multiplicity of institutions and deposit types and to omit the international complexities. Accordingly, this exposition makes use of a simplified schematic framework, the essential elements of which are briefly summarized in the following section. A more detailed description is provided in appendix A.[1]

A Schematic Framework for the Analysis of the Money Market

The balance sheet of the U.S. monetary authorities includes, on the liability side, the amount of currency in circulation, *CUR*; the total

1. Readers can skip this appendix unless they need further detail about the framework or want to verify the analytical conclusions derived from it.

reserves of commercial banks, RT; and the deposit balance of the rest of the government held at the Federal Reserve, Dep^G. On the asset side the balance sheet includes borrowing by the commercial banks at the Federal Reserve discount window, BOR; the security portfolio of the monetary authorities, S^{MA}; and the amount of Federal Reserve float, Flt.[2] From one period to the next, changes in the items on this balance sheet must satisfy the identity,

$$\Delta BOR + \Delta S^{MA} + \Delta Flt - \Delta CUR - \Delta RT - \Delta Dep^G \equiv 0. \tag{2-1}$$

The total reserves of the banks are predominantly required reserves, RR; but the banking system as a whole also holds a highly variable amount of excess reserves, RX. Unborrowed reserves, RU, are defined as total reserves less discount-window borrowing. The monetary base, B, is defined as the sum of total reserves and currency in circulation. In addition to the identity (1), therefore, changes in the reserve aggregates always satisfy the following three identities:

$$\Delta RT \equiv \Delta RR + \Delta RX, \tag{2-2}$$

$$\Delta RU \equiv \Delta RT - \Delta BOR, \tag{2-3}$$

$$\Delta B \equiv \Delta RT + \Delta CUR. \tag{2-4}$$

To keep the schematic framework as simple as possible, only one type of financial intermediary is considered. These "banks" are assumed to issue only one type of deposit, D, to the nonbank sectors of the economy. The money stock, M, is therefore defined here simply as the sum of currency and the single type of deposit. This definition adds a fifth identity to the schematic framework:

$$\Delta M \equiv \Delta CUR + \Delta D. \tag{2-5}$$

The "demand" side of the processes determining the money stock depends on the asset-holding behavior of nonbanks. The framework incorporates conventional assumptions for both currency and deposits: nonbanks are assumed to hold more money if the nominal value of economic activity increases and to hold less if short-term interest rates rise. In addition, to facilitate an analysis of the consequences of changes

2. Table A-1 in appendix A shows the balance sheet explicitly. The phrase "U.S. monetary authorities" refers to the Federal Reserve System plus certain monetary accounts of the U.S. Treasury. Hereafter I use "monetary authorities" and "the Federal Reserve" interchangeably.

in money demand that are *not* attributable to changes in nominal GNP and changes in interest rates, the schematic framework includes a representation of autonomous or stochastic shifts in the demand for the two components of money.

Even at the highly simplified level of this framework, three types of private-sector behavior influence the "supply" of money: the banks' holdings of required reserves, the banks' holdings of excess reserves, and the amount of the banks' borrowing at the discount window. As explained in appendix A, each type of behavior may be described as having a systematic component (susceptible to prediction, although not perfect prediction, by the Federal Reserve and other analysts of the money market) and a stochastic component (much less susceptible to prediction). For example, the banks' borrowing from the Federal Reserve is assumed to vary positively with the spread between the short-term market interest rate and the Federal Reserve's discount rate; but borrowing is also modeled as including a stochastic component not related to interest rates.

The schematic framework omits, even in outline form, many crucial aspects of the financial behavior of nonbanks and financial intermediaries. It is thus not an acceptable analytical framework for discussing the behavior of financial markets as a whole. Nor is it adequate for analyzing the most important interrelations between financial markets and goods markets. The schema here deals merely with key relations determining the stock of money—that is, what is conventionally termed the "money market." Even in its treatment of the money market, moreover, this schema suppresses some behavioral and institutional complications that are significant in real life. For example, the schema ignores lagged responses in the behavior of private-sector decisionmakers and does not deal in a sophisticated way with the formation of expectations in the private sector. It assumes "contemporaneous" rather than "two-week lagged" reserve accounting (even though the latter prevailed in practice during 1968–82).[3]

Because of its severe limitations, the expositional framework here can be used to derive only a narrow range of valid conclusions. Accord-

3. A similar exposition of the essential elements of a "money-market model" is contained in several recent papers by Peter Tinsley and other members of the Federal Reserve Board staff, and that work in turn has extensive antecedents in the journal literature (see appendix A). I have drawn heavily on such sources in preparing this book. Chapter 6 contains a discussion of reserve-accounting procedures.

ingly, I have been careful to emphasize only those robust inferences that would also emerge from more complex and realistic frameworks.

Despite these limitations, the schema does successfully incorporate the most essential fact about the nexus of money supply and demand: money is determined by Federal Reserve decisions *and* by nonpolicy factors that are outside the control of the Federal Reserve.

The money supply and demand process—indeed, the entire financial system—is like an inverted pyramid balanced on a small tip. The tip of the pyramid is the balance sheet of the monetary authorities; it supports all the upper layers of the structure, including the money stock in any of its conventional definitions. Other things being equal, an incremental expansion of the Federal Reserve's balance sheet will stimulate an expansion of the pyramid as a whole, and vice versa for an incremental contraction. Federal Reserve policy decisions are thus an extremely important determinant of changes in the money stock and other financial magnitudes. Over a longer period, measured in quarters or years rather than weeks or months, Federal Reserve decisions are a primary determinant.

This importance of the Federal Reserve's balance sheet is widely understood, even by noneconomists. What is less well understood is the complex and elastic relations between the Federal Reserve balance sheet and the balance sheets of the private-sector intermediaries in the financial system. The inverted pyramid is a flexible rather than rigid structure, capable of substantial changes in size and shape that are not directly attributable to changes in the small tip at the bottom controlled by the Federal Reserve. Because of this flexibility and adaptability, the "multipliers" linking a change in the Federal Reserve balance sheet to changes in the money stock and to other financial magnitudes are uncertain and subject to significant variation.

Alternative Operating Procedures for the Federal Reserve

The Federal Reserve has command over several policy *instruments*. It makes decisions about, and takes actions to adjust, the "settings" on its instruments. A *policy action* is an alteration of the setting on one or more instruments.

A financial variable is a *potential* instrument if the Federal Reserve could control it precisely. A variable is an *actual* instrument if the

Federal Reserve can control it precisely and if in fact the Federal Reserve does control it precisely.

In this schematic framework the Federal Reserve discount rate, r^d, and the reserve-requirement ratio applicable to the banks' deposits, h, are actual policy instruments. In addition, the Federal Reserve can choose one other financial variable to use as its primary actual instrument for implementing policy. Five variables in this framework are *potential* candidates to be this primary instrument. One of these, the short-term interest rate, represented by the federal funds rate, r^{ff}, is a financial "price." The other four variables—the Federal Reserve's security portfolio, S^{MA}; total reserves, RT; unborrowed reserves, RU; and the monetary base, B—are financial "quantities" on the balance sheet of the monetary authorities. Once the Federal Reserve chooses one of these five candidates to serve as its main actual instrument, the other four cannot be actual instruments.[4]

In this schematic framework, therefore, the Federal Reserve can choose among five alternative operating regimes when implementing monetary policy. For convenience, they can be labeled *portfolio regime, base regime, total-reserves regime, unborrowed-reserves regime,* and *funds-rate regime* according to whether the Federal Reserve selects as its main instrument, respectively, the security portfolio, the monetary base, total reserves, unborrowed reserves, or the federal funds rate. (In addition to its primary instrument, the Federal Reserve would also use the discount rate and the reserve-requirement ratio as instruments in each of the five regimes.)

In real life the Federal Reserve has available an analogous set of options when selecting its operating procedures. The schematic framework described here thus faithfully represents the problem of instrument choice facing the Federal Reserve.

Neither in real life nor in the schematic framework can the money stock be an instrument of monetary policy: the Federal Reserve cannot control it precisely from one short-run period to the next. To be sure, the Federal Reserve can try to control the movements of the money stock as closely as possible. In that event, however, conceptual clarity calls for describing money as a *target* variable.

Few if any policymakers and economists perceive the money stock as a variable to be pursued in its own right as a final goal of monetary

4. For further discussion of this point see appendix A.

policy. The *ultimate targets* of policy are such variables as the volume of output, the level of employment, and the average price level. If the Federal Reserve chooses to aim at the money stock as a target variable, therefore, the rationale for doing so presumably rests on money being a useful surrogate for the ultimate targets of policy. Under such circumstances, the money stock is an *intermediate-target* variable.

A decision by the Federal Reserve to use money as an intermediate target is logically separable from its choice among the five operating regimes or procedures. If thought desirable, the Federal Reserve can select the money stock as an intermediate-target variable regardless of its choice of procedure.

When discussing Federal Reserve policy, it is essential to distinguish between *instrument choice* and decisions about *instrument variation.* Instrument choice is the selection of an operating regime. Given the choice of procedure, decisions about instrument variation determine how the settings of the instruments are altered over time. Because the Federal Reserve typically makes major decisions only at periodic meetings and because the settings on instruments may not be reconsidered in the intervals between meetings, the problem of instrument choice is not trivial. Alternative selections for the operating regime can produce substantially different outcomes for target variables in the short run. Nonetheless, over a longer run the choice of regime tends to be much less important than the discretionary decisions about instrument variation.

The Consequences of Nonpolicy Disturbances under Alternative Operating Regimes

In this schematic framework unexpected variations in nonpolicy factors can originate from eight sources: changes in float, in the government's deposit balance, in required reserves, in excess reserves, in discount-window borrowing, in currency demand, in deposit demand, and in the nominal value of economic activity. In real life the Federal Reserve confronts sizable, short-run variations in each of these areas at one time or another. In what follows, *unexpected* variations in these nonpolicy factors will be referred to as "nonpolicy disturbances."[5]

Regardless of the operating regime used by the Federal Reserve,

5. The distinction between expected and unexpected variations in the nonpolicy determinants of the money stock is discussed in appendix A.

nonpolicy disturbances inevitably have some sort of consequences for some financial variables. The relevant issue for monetary policy is not whether but rather *where* these consequences will manifest themselves. When any given disturbance occurs, it must be channeled in one direction or another, thereby causing a change in one or more financial variables. The particular "destinations" of the effects of the disturbance—which variables it influences, and by how much—differ under alternative operating regimes. From the perspective of the Federal Reserve, therefore, it becomes important to know, for each type of disturbance, which operating regime is associated with the least troublesome consequences.

A presumption exists that, regardless of the Federal Reserve's operating procedure, an unexpected nonpolicy disturbance will have minor consequences and can therefore be ignored if the disturbance is small (in relation to other money-market variables) and transitory (quickly reversed). Conversely, if large, persistent, or both large and persistent, a disturbance is presumed to be potentially troublesome. The discussion that follows in the first instance analyzes each type of disturbance without regard for its typical size or duration. The important question of the relative sizes and durations of disturbances is taken up after each disturbance has been examined in turn.

The analysis focuses on the consequences of each type of disturbance for the money stock, M, and for short-term interest rates, r^{ff}. The effects on money are obviously of special interest if the Federal Reserve uses the money stock as an intermediate-target variable. Even if the Federal Reserve does not use money as an intermediate target, the analysis is germane for the conduct of policy. Movements in short-term interest rates and in the money stock are primary channels through which nonpolicy disturbances in the money market (and Federal Reserve policy actions) are transmitted to the remainder of the economy, thereby eventually influencing the ultimate targets of monetary policy.

Float and the Government's Deposit Balance

Unexpected changes in float and in the government's deposit balance at the Federal Reserve are two types of nonpolicy disturbance whose consequences are simple to summarize and to grasp. As a first example, therefore, consider what happens to the money stock and the federal funds rate following an unpredicted increase in float.[6]

6. The consequences of an unexpected decrease in the government's deposit balance are identical to the consequences of an unexpected increase of the same magnitude in float.

Table 2-1. *Consequences of an Unexpected Increase in Float or an Unexpected Decrease in the Government's Deposit Balance*[a]

Endogenous variable affected	*Operating procedure for monetary policy*				
	Portfolio regime	*Base regime*	*Total-reserves regime*	*Unborrowed-reserves regime*	*Funds-rate regime*
Money stock, M	M increases	No effect	No effect	No effect	No effect
Short-term interest rate, r^{ff}	r^{ff} decreases	No effect	No effect	No effect	**r^{ff} is an exogenous instrument**
Security portfolio of the monetary authorities, S^{MA}	**S^{MA} is an exogenous instrument**	S^{MA} is reduced by the amount of the increase in float	S^{MA} is reduced by the amount of the increase in float	S^{MA} is reduced by the amount of the increase in float	S^{MA} is reduced by the amount of the increase in float

Source: Appendix A, table A-4.

a. The variable M is currency in circulation plus deposits at banks; r^{ff}, the federal funds rate; and S^{MA}, the portfolio of securities used by the Federal Reserve in open-market operations.

If the Federal Reserve is conducting policy with the portfolio regime, it will have already decided on its instrument setting for the portfolio and hence will keep S^{MA} unchanged as the unexpected increase in float occurs. Total reserves (and excess reserves) are therefore increased. With the banks' demand for reserves unchanged at the existing level of the funds rate, that rate must fall to induce the banks to hold the larger quantity of reserves. In response to the decline in interest rates, the demand for money, and hence the money stock itself, increases. This change in money is undesirable from the perspective of policymakers if the Federal Reserve is pursuing a money-stock target. Even if the Federal Reserve attaches importance only to variables that are the ultimate targets of policy, the fall in r^{ff} and the increase in M are undesirable developments. (Whether the adverse changes in r^{ff} and M have minor or significant effects on ultimate targets depends on, among other things, whether the increase in float persists and whether private expectations attribute the changes in the money market to an unexpected nonpolicy disturbance or to a change of policy by the Federal Reserve.)

In sharp contrast, the unexpected increase in float does not have adverse consequences under any of the other four operating regimes. In each of those other regimes, the surprise in Flt induces the Federal Reserve to conduct offsetting open-market operations for the purpose of keeping its primary instrument at the policy setting determined at the outset of the short-run period. Regardless of whether that instrument is B, RT, RU, or r^{ff}, the Federal Reserve sells an amount of securities sufficient to offset exactly the increase in float. Hence no change in interest rates is necessary under the base regime, the total-reserves regime, and the unborrowed-reserves regime to clear an imbalance in the market for immediately available funds. And under those three quantity regimes and under the funds-rate regime, the money stock remains undisturbed.

To state the same facts another way, under every operating regime except the portfolio regime the variable S^{MA} is the sole "destination" of (the only endogenous variable to be influenced by) unexpected changes in Flt and Dep^G. In effect, the Federal Reserve portfolio absorbs these nonpolicy surprises and thereby "insulates" variables like the money stock from their consequences. Under the portfolio regime, on the other hand, these nonpolicy surprises must find an outlet somewhere else; hence short-term interest rates and the money stock, among other variables, are forced to adjust. Because the money stock and interest

Table 2-2. *Consequences of an Unexpected Increase in the Demand for Excess Reserves or an Unexpected Increase in Required Reserves*[a]

Endogenous variable affected	*Operating procedure for monetary policy*				
	Portfolio regime	*Base regime*	*Total-reserves regime*	*Unborrowed-reserves regime*	*Funds-rate regime*
Money stock, *M*	*M* declines but less than under any of the other quantity regimes	*M* declines less than under the total-reserves regime, more than under the portfolio regime, and (probably) more than under the unborrowed-reserves regime	*M* declines by a large multiple of the unexpected increase in *RX* or *RR*; the decline is greater than under any of the other operating regimes	*M* declines, less than under the total-reserves regime, more than under the portfolio regime, and (probably) less than under the base regime	No effect
Short-term interest rate, r^{ff}	r^{ff} rises, but less than under any of the other quantity regimes	r^{ff} rises, less than under the total-reserves regime, more than under the portfolio regime, and (probably) more than under the unborrowed-reserves regime	r^{ff} rises by more than under any of the other operating regimes	r^{ff} rises, less than under the total-reserves regime, more than under the portfolio regime, and (probably) less than under the base regime	**r^{ff} is an exogenous instrument**
Security portfolio of the monetary authorities, S^{MA}	**S^{MA} is an exogenous instrument**	S^{MA} is reduced (by an amount equal to the increase in *BOR* induced by the rise in r^{ff})	S^{MA} is reduced (by an amount equal to the increase in *BOR* plus the reduction in nonbanks' holdings of *CUR*)	S^{MA} is reduced (by an amount equal to the reduction in nonbanks' holdings of *CUR* induced by the rise in r^{ff})	S^{MA} is increased by the amount of the unexpected increase in *RX* or *RR*

Source: Appendix A, table A-5.

a. The variable *M* is currency in circulation plus deposits at banks; r^{ff}, the federal funds rate; S^{MA}, the portfolio of securities used by the Federal Reserve in open-market operations; *BOR*, discount-window borrowing; *CUR*, currency in circulation; *RX*, excess reserves; and *RR*, required reserves.

rates change under the portfolio regime, moreover, the original disturbance is transmitted to still further destinations in the rest of the economy.

Table 2-1 summarizes the consequences of an unexpected increase in float or an unexpected reduction in the government's deposit balance under the alternative operating regimes. Subsequent tables provide an analogous comparison of the consequences of other types of nonpolicy disturbances.

As the above discussion suggests, in principle the portfolio regime is the worst operating procedure for the Federal Reserve to be using at the time of unexpected changes in float and in the government's deposit balance. Judged only from the perspective of the consequences of these two types of nonpolicy disturbances, any one of the other four regimes can serve equally well to channel the disturbances into an untroublesome destination.

Excess Reserves and Required Reserves

I next consider an unexpected increase in the banks' demand for reserve balances at the Federal Reserve. The consequences of an unpredicted change in the need to hold required reserves are identical to the consequences of an unpredicted change of the same sign and magnitude in the banks' demand for excess reserves (see appendix A). For brevity, therefore, I discuss only an unexpected increase in excess reserves.

If the Federal Reserve conducts policy with the funds-rate regime, it is induced to carry out open-market purchases to prevent the funds rate from rising above its predetermined instrument setting. The amount of the purchases made is just sufficient to provide the incremental amount of reserves demanded by the banks. With no change in the funds rate, the money stock remains at the value expected by the Federal Reserve before the surprise surge in excess reserves.

Under all four of the other regimes (the quantity regimes), the unexpected increase in excess reserves puts upward pressure on the funds rate. That rise in interest rates in turn produces declines in the demand for currency and for deposits, and hence an unplanned and undesired decline in the money stock itself (see table 2-2).

The greatest increase in the funds rate and the largest fall in the money stock occur under the total-reserves regime. In this case, to keep the

Table 2-3. *Consequences of an Unexpected Increase in Discount-Window Borrowing*[a]

Endogenous variable affected	*Operating procedure for monetary policy*				
	Portfolio regime	*Base regime*	*Total-reserves regime*	*Unborrowed-reserves regime*	*Funds-rate regime*
Money stock, M	M increases, but less than under the unborrowed-reserves regime	No effect	No effect	M increases	No effect
Short-term interest rate, r^{ff}	r^{ff} falls, but less than under the unborrowed-reserves regime	No effect	No effect	r^{ff} falls	**r^{ff} is an exogenous instrument**
Security portfolio of the monetary authorities, S^{MA}	**S^{MA} is an exogenous instrument**	S^{MA} is reduced by the amount of the unexpected increase in borrowing	S^{MA} is reduced by the amount of the unexpected increase in borrowing	S^{MA} is increased by an amount equal to the increase in nonbanks' holdings of CUR induced by the rise in r^{ff}	S^{MA} is reduced by the amount of the unexpected increase in borrowing

Source: Appendix A, table A-6.

a. The variable M is currency in circulation plus deposits at banks; r^{ff}, the federal funds rate; S^{MA}, the portfolio of securities used by the Federal Reserve in open-market operations; and CUR, currency in circulation.

quantity of total reserves from rising above the instrument setting chosen before the disturbance, the Federal Reserve must carry out open-market sales of securities; these sales must be sufficient to offset an increase in discount-window borrowing and a fall in nonbanks' demand for currency (both of which are induced by the rise in the funds rate). The resulting fall in the money stock is a large multiple of the unexpected increase in the demand for excess reserves.

Among the four quantity regimes, the smallest increase in the funds rate and the smallest decline in the money stock occur under the portfolio regime. Given the nature of this regime, the disturbance cannot induce any change in the Federal Reserve's security portfolio. Increases in discount-window borrowing and reductions in currency holdings are permitted to raise total reserves. Hence the rise in the funds rate and the fall in the money stock necessary to accommodate the disturbance are much smaller than those resulting under the total-reserves regime.

The consequences under the base regime and the unborrowed-reserves regime fall in between the large changes under the total-reserves regime and the modest changes under the portfolio regime. The probable outcome is a larger rise in the funds rate and a larger fall in the money stock under the base regime than under the unborrowed-reserves regime.

At the time unexpected changes occur in banks' demands for reserves, therefore, the Federal Reserve is unambiguously worst off if it is conducting policy with a total-reserves regime. The preferred regime for handling this type of disturbance is the funds-rate regime; the Federal Reserve portfolio then fully absorbs any unexpected changes in reserve demands and thus prevents the disturbances from influencing the money stock. In contrast, under the total-reserves regime the money stock becomes an important destination of the disturbance. To a lesser but still significant extent, the money stock is a destination of the disturbance under each of the other quantity regimes.

Discount-Window Borrowing

The nonpolicy disturbances discussed above originate in what is conventionally termed the supply side of the money market. Changes in discount-window borrowing that cannot be predicted by the Federal Reserve are still another type of supply disturbance. Table 2-3 summarizes the consequences of an unexpected surge in borrowing under the five alternative operating regimes.

Under the funds-rate regime, the total-reserves regime, and the base regime, an unexpected increase in borrowing would alter the predetermined setting for the main policy instrument in the absence of offsetting open-market operations. Hence under these three regimes, merely to prevent a change in its instrument setting, the Federal Reserve is induced to sell securities from its portfolio to match, dollar for dollar, the unexpected increase in *BOR*. In effect, the entire impact of the disturbance is absorbed into the variable S^{MA}. Because of this absorption, the money stock remains undisturbed.

If the Federal Reserve conducts policy with either the portfolio regime or the unborrowed-reserves regime, however, the disturbance in borrowing does get transmitted to troublesome destinations. The increase in *BOR* raises total reserves and induces a fall in the funds rate. These changes in turn generate increases in the demands for deposits and for currency, and hence increases in the money stock. The fall in r^{ff} and the rise in *M* are larger under the unborrowed-reserves regime than under the portfolio regime.

The analytical results summarized in table 2-3 thus lead to the conclusion that surprises in discount-window borrowing are most troublesome when the Federal Reserve conducts policy with the unborrowed-reserves regime. The consequences for policy are still adverse under the portfolio regime, but less so. Judged only from the perspective of how well they handle unexpected changes in borrowing, the other three regimes serve equally well to insulate the money stock (and the rest of the economy).

Autonomous Changes in Deposit Demand

The remaining types of nonpolicy disturbances to be analyzed in this schematic framework originate in what is conventionally termed the demand side of the money market. The first of these is an unexpected change in the "autonomous" component of deposit demand. Table 2-4 compares the consequences of this type of disturbance under the five operating regimes.

If the Federal Reserve conducts policy with the funds-rate regime, r^{ff} is prevented from rising by induced open-market purchases of securities. For every dollar of unexpected increase in deposit demand, the Federal Reserve supplies exactly enough reserves to satisfy the increment in required reserves. The amount of deposits outstanding and also the money stock itself rise by the full amount (dollar for dollar) of the increased autonomous demand.

Under the total-reserves regime the consequences are dramatically different. The funds rate rises in response to the unexpected increase in deposit demand and the associated increase in required reserves. To keep total reserves unchanged at the predetermined instrument setting, furthermore, the Federal Reserve must actually sell securities to the private sector to offset induced increases in discount-window borrowing and induced reductions in currency holdings. The rise in r^{ff} is thus even sharper than it would have been in the absence of the open-market sales. The increase in r^{ff} under this regime is larger than under any of the other regimes. In fact, it is sufficiently large to induce an actual *decline* in the money stock.

If the Federal Reserve uses the portfolio regime for implementing policy, r^{ff} rises in response to the disturbance. This rise, however, is smaller than under any of the other three quantity regimes. Hence the money stock, although increasing less than under the funds-rate regime, still rises by a substantial fraction of the increment in autonomous deposit demand.

The base regime and the unborrowed-reserves regime produce outcomes for the rise in r^{ff} and the change in M that fall in between those associated with the total-reserves and the portfolio regimes (see table 2-4). Under plausible assumptions discussed in appendix A, the rise in M is larger under the unborrowed-reserves regime than under the base regime.

To assess which of the five regimes directs a disturbance in autonomous deposit demand to the least troublesome destination, one must understand clearly the hypothesized nature of this disturbance. The increase in deposit demand is not attributable to unexpectedly strong activity in goods markets (increases in goods output, goods prices, or some of both) and hence to an induced increase in the transactions demand for money. Rather, by definition the disturbance is a shift in asset preferences for given levels of interest rates, nominal income, and wealth: that is, an increased demand for deposits matched by an offsetting lower demand for other assets (for example, for bonds or for liquid assets not included in the money stock).

Given the nature of this disturbance, the least troublesome destination for it is the quantity of deposits itself. The preferable outcome, in other words, is for deposits and hence the money stock to increase by the full

Table 2-4. *Consequences of an Unexpected Increase in Autonomous Deposit Demand*[a]

Endogenous variable affected	*Operating procedure for monetary policy*				
	Portfolio regime	*Base regime*	*Total-reserves regime*	*Unborrowed-reserves regime*	*Funds-rate regime*
Money stock, *M*	*M* increases, but less than under the funds-rate regime	*M* increases, less than under the portfolio regime and (probably) less than under the unborrowed-reserves regime	*M* declines	*M* increases, less than under the portfolio regime and (probably) more than under the base regime	*M* increases dollar for dollar with the unexpected increase in autonomous deposit demand
Short-term interest rate, r^{ff}	r^{ff} rises, but less than under any of the other "quantity" regimes	r^{ff} rises, less than under the total-reserves regime, more than under the portfolio regime, and (probably) more than under the unborrowed-reserves regime	r^{ff} rises by more than under any of the other operating regimes	r^{ff} rises, less than under the total-reserves regime, more than under the portfolio regime, and (probably) less than under the base regime	**r^{ff} is an exogenous instrument**
Security portfolio of the monetary authorities, S^{MA}	**S^{MA} is an exogenous instrument**	S^{MA} is reduced by an amount equal to the increase in *BOR* induced by the rise in r^{ff}	S^{MA} is reduced by an amount equal to the increase in *BOR* plus the reduction in nonbanks' holdings of *CUR*	S^{MA} is reduced by an amount equal to the reduction in nonbanks' holdings of *CUR* induced by the rise in r^{ff}	S^{MA} is increased by an amount equal to the product of the reserve-requirement ratio and the increment in deposit demand

Source: Appendix A, table A-7.

a. The variable *M* is currency in circulation plus deposits at banks; r^{ff}, the federal funds rate; S^{MA}, the portfolio of securities used by the Federal Reserve in open-market operations; *BOR*, discount-window borrowing; and *CUR*, currency in circulation.

amount of the autonomous shift in asset preferences, thereby preventing the increase in interest rates that must otherwise occur. The smaller the increase in interest rates, the better. At any rate, the Federal Reserve should reach that conclusion if its concern is with such variables as inflation and output. Increases in interest rates induced by autonomous shifts in asset preferences can have adverse consequences for the best attainable combination of output growth and inflation; increases in the money stock that accommodate such shifts cannot.

The analysis of unexpected changes in autonomous deposit demand summarized in table 2-4 thus leads to the conclusion that the worst regime for coping with such disturbances is the total-reserves regime. More specifically, the five regimes can be ranked—in order from the worst to the best—as the total-reserves regime, the base regime, the unborrowed-reserves regime, the portfolio regime, and the funds-rate regime.

Autonomous Changes in Currency Demand

Table 2-5 compares the consequences under the alternative regimes of an unexpected increase in the autonomous component of currency demand. (Like the preceding illustration concerned with autonomous deposit demand, this disturbance arises from a shift of asset preferences for given levels of interest rates, nominal income, and wealth. By definition, nonbanks increase their currency holdings and correspondingly lower their demand for other financial assets such as bonds or nonmoney liquid assets.)[7]

Under three of the operating procedures—the funds-rate, unborrowed-reserves, and total-reserves regimes—this nonpolicy disturbance is fully accommodated in the stock of currency. That is, each of the regimes permits a dollar-for-dollar increase of currency holdings, and hence also of the money stock, in response to the incrementally higher demand. In effect, the Federal Reserve "automatically" supplies the additional amount of currency as it carries out the induced open-market purchases of securities required to keep the main instrument in these regimes at its predetermined setting.

7. Still another type of nonpolicy disturbance would be a shift by nonbanks into currency matched by a corresponding decrease in deposits included in the money stock. This asset shift can be analyzed in the framework here by, in effect, combining the results in tables 2-4 and 2-5 (tables A-7 and A-8 in appendix A).

Table 2-5. *Consequences of an Unexpected Increase in Autonomous Currency Demand*[a]

Endogenous variable affected	*Operating procedure for monetary policy*				
	Portfolio regime	*Base regime*	*Total-reserves regime*	*Unborrowed-reserves regime*	*Funds-rate regime*
Money stock, M	M increases by a fraction of the unexpected increase in currency demand or declines slightly. If M declines, the fall is smaller than under the base regime	M declines	M increases dollar for dollar with the unexpected increase in autonomous currency demand	M increases dollar for dollar with the unexpected increase in autonomous currency demand	M increases dollar for dollar with the unexpected increase in autonomous currency demand
Short-term interest rate, r^{ff}	r^{ff} rises but less than under the base regime	r^{ff} rises	No effect	No effect	**r^{ff} is an exogenous instrument**
Security portfolio of the monetary authorities, S^{MA}	**S^{MA} is an exogenous instrument**	S^{MA} is reduced by an amount equal to the increase in *BOR* induced by the rise in r^{ff}	S^{MA} is increased by the amount of the unexpected increase in *CUR*	S^{MA} is increased by the amount of the unexpected increase in *CUR*	S^{MA} is increased by the amount of the unexpected increase in *CUR*

Source: Appendix A, table A-8.

a. The variable M is currency in circulation plus deposits at banks; r^{ff}, the federal funds rate; S^{MA}, the portfolio of securities used by the Federal Reserve in open-market operations; *BOR*, discount-window borrowing; and *CUR*, currency in circulation.

Under the two remaining procedures, however, the unexpected increase in currency demand is not fully accommodated and therefore spills over to influence other variables. In particular, the disturbance pushes interest rates upward. The rise in the funds rate is larger under the base regime than the portfolio regime. In fact, r^{ff} rises enough under the base regime to induce a contraction in the money stock. The money stock may fractionally increase, or decline slightly, under the portfolio regime; if the money stock declines, the amount of the decline is smaller than that occurring under the base regime.

The least troublesome destination for an unexpected increase in autonomous currency demand is the quantity of currency itself. The funds-rate, unborrowed-reserves, and total-reserves regimes are therefore equally effective in coping with this type of disturbance. The worst procedure for handling such disturbances is the base regime.

Unexpected Changes in Aggregate Demand

The final type of nonpolicy disturbance in this schematic framework is an unexpected change in the nominal value of economic activity (aggregate demand). This type of disturbance manifests itself through the demand side of the money market. It is, however, quite unlike the two previous demand disturbances. Those two disturbances were shifts in asset preferences for given levels of interest rates, income, and wealth. This type of disturbance occurs with unchanged asset preferences; the demand for money changes *because* income and wealth are changing.

Indeed, an unexpected increase in aggregate demand is a qualitatively different type of disturbance than all of those previously considered. It originates outside financial markets, somewhere in the goods markets or labor markets in the rest of the economy. Financial markets react to it, and through effects transmitted back to the real sectors can influence the ultimate strength and distribution of its effects. In contrast, each of the other disturbances previously discussed may be said to originate within the financial markets.[8]

To ask which Federal Reserve operating regime copes best with an unexpected increase in aggregate demand is to ask which regime pro-

8. With a less limited analytical framework than the one used here, one would not characterize an unexpected change in aggregate demand as a single disturbance, but instead would identify a variety of different disturbances originating in goods and labor markets that cause an unexpected change in aggregate demand.

Table 2-6. *Consequences of an Unexpected Increase in Nominal Economic Activity*[a,b]

	Operating procedure for monetary policy				
Endogenous variable affected	*Portfolio regime*	*Base regime*	*Total-reserves regime*	*Unborrowed-reserves regime*	*Funds-rate regime*
Money stock, M	M increases more than under the base regime	M increases less than under the portfolio regime	M increases less than under the unborrowed-reserves regime	M increases more than under the total-reserves regime	M increases by a larger amount than under any of the other regimes
Short-term interest rate, r^{ff}	r^{ff} rises less than under the base regime	r^{ff} rises more than under the portfolio regime	r^{ff} rises more than under the unborrowed-reserves regime	r^{ff} rises less than under the total-reserves regime	**r^{ff} is an exogenous instrument**
Security portfolio of the monetary authorities, S^{MA}	**S^{MA} is an exogenous instrument**	S^{MA} is reduced	S^{MA} is probably reduced	S^{MA} may either be reduced or increased	S^{MA} is increased

Source: Appendix A, table A-9.

a. The unexpected increase in nominal economic activity is assumed to be caused by disturbances originating outside the financial markets.

b. The variable M is currency in circulation plus deposits at banks; r^{ff}, the federal funds rate; and S^{MA}, the portfolio of securities used by the Federal Reserve in open-market operations.

cesses the effects of such a disturbance in financial markets and feeds financial consequences back to the real economy in the way that has the least troublesome consequences for variables that are ultimate targets. Table 2-6, which is organized like the previous tables, does not show the consequences for those variables. But inferences about those consequences can be drawn from the effects on interest rates and the money stock.

Consider first the effects of a surprise surge in aggregate demand when the Federal Reserve conducts policy with the funds-rate regime. Because the funds rate is the main policy instrument, the Federal Reserve does not permit the funds rate to rise in response to the unexpected disturbance. To keep the funds rate from rising, the Federal Reserve must carry out open-market purchases of securities; these in turn increase total reserves. The money stock is thus able to rise by the full amount of the increased transactions demand for money. In the absence of any rise in the funds rate and with money allowed to increase in order to accommodate fully the increased demand, the financial markets in effect pose no resistance to the disturbance originating in the real sectors of the economy.

Under all four quantity regimes, on the other hand, some rise in the funds rate does occur. This in turn helps to dampen the rise in money demand and hence in the money stock itself. The increase in interest rates also helps to restrain expenditures in the goods markets directly. Under the four quantity regimes, therefore, the financial markets transmit back to the real economy some restraining forces that work against the initial disturbance to aggregate demand.

Regardless of the operating procedures followed by the Federal Reserve, under plausible assumptions the financial markets are not able to provide enough resistance to prevent the initial disturbance from causing some increase in prices or output. Hence it is reasonable to presume that the more resistance provided by financial markets—in particular, the greater the rise in the funds rate and the smaller the rise in the money stock—the better will be the outcome for the economy.[9]

How do the four quantity regimes compare with each other in

9. The statements in this paragraph do not take into account the possibility that some types of disturbances originating in the real sectors of the economy may be inherently favorable (for example, unexpected improvements in labor productivity due to new inventions or better labor-management relations). For such favorable disturbances, the generalizations in the text are inapplicable. See also note 8 above.

promoting a rise in the funds rate and dampening the increase in the money stock? Unambiguously, the total-reserves regime always performs better than the unborrowed-reserves regime. It is also unambiguous that the base regime always performs better than the portfolio regime.

To determine the relative rankings of all four quantity regimes, one must have information about the magnitudes as well as the signs of behavioral responses in the private sector. Appendix A presents a discussion of this issue. To summarize: the degree of rise in the funds rate and the extent of dampening of the money stock resulting from an unexpected increase in aggregate demand are probably largest under the total-reserves regime and next largest under the base regime. The smallest rise in the funds rate and dampening of the money stock probably occurs under the unborrowed-reserves regime. The size of the responses under the portfolio regime probably falls in between those under the base regime and the unborrowed-reserves regime.

The most important point to emerge from the analysis of this type of disturbance is the inferiority of the funds-rate regime. This is essentially the same conclusion emphasized by William Poole and by the economists who subsequently elaborated on Poole's analysis.[10]

10. See William Poole, "Optimal Choice of Monetary Policy Instruments in a Simple Stochastic Macro Model," *Quarterly Journal of Economics*, vol. 84 (May 1970), pp. 197–216; Stephen F. LeRoy, "Efficient Use of Current Information in Short-Run Monetary Control," Special Studies Paper 66, Board of Governors of the Federal Reserve System, Division of Research and Statistics (September 1975); and Stephen F. LeRoy and David E. Lindsey, "Determining the Monetary Instrument: A Diagrammatic Exposition," *American Economic Review*, vol. 68 (December 1978), pp. 929–34.

CHAPTER THREE

Which Operating Procedure Performs Best?

THE PRECEDING ANALYSIS of the consequences of nonpolicy disturbances under alternative operating procedures leads naturally to the issue of instrument choice itself. Which of the available operating regimes should the Federal Reserve select to conduct monetary policy?

No Regime Dominates for All Nonpolicy Disturbances

Table 3-1 presents an overview of the results discussed in chapter 2. For each type of disturbance (the rows in the table), the five regimes are ranked relative to each other. The regime, or regimes, under which a particular disturbance is directed to the least troublesome destinations is given a grade of "A"; the worst regime is graded "F." (The rankings in the table are valid only across the rows, and hence the table should be read horizontally, one row at a time.)

Table 3-1 makes clear a fundamental fact: no one operating regime performs best for all types of nonpolicy disturbances. This fact in turn has far-reaching implications for Federal Reserve policy.

All the types of disturbance analyzed in this schematic framework occur in real life. Moreover, the different types can occur simultaneously. The Federal Reserve attempts to predict the movements of the relevant variables ex ante, and to identify unexpected disturbances as they occur. But the ability of the Federal Reserve to predict ex ante is severely limited. And the Federal Reserve cannot identify disturbances precisely and promptly at the time they first appear.

The beginning of wisdom about the conduct of monetary policy, therefore, is to acknowledge an awkward conclusion. Whatever operating regime the Federal Reserve uses to implement policy, the short-

Table 3-1. *Performance of Alternative Operating Regimes in Directing Nonpolicy Disturbances to Least Troublesome Destinations*[a]

Type of disturbance (unexpected change in behavior of private sectors of the economy)	*Operating procedure for monetary policy*				
	Portfolio regime	*Base regime*	*Total-reserves regime*	*Unborrowed-reserves regime*	*Funds-rate regime*
Supply side of money market					
Float	F	A	A	A	A
Government deposit balance	F	A	A	A	A
Excess reserves	B	D	F	C	A
Required reserves	B	D	F	C	A
Discount-window borrowing	D	A	A	F	A
Demand side of money market					
Shift in deposit demand	B	D	F	C	A
Shift in currency demand	D	F	A	A	A
External to financial markets	C	B	A	D	F

Source: Tables 2-1 through 2-6 and appendix A.

a. For a particular nonpolicy disturbance, identified in a row of the table, each regime is ranked relative to the others. "A" indicates the preferred regime for that disturbance—preferred in the sense that the disturbance has least troublesome consequences for the policy objectives of the Federal Reserve. "B," "C," and "D" indicate, respectively, the second, third, and fourth best regimes. The regime under which a disturbance has the most troublesome consequences is marked "F." When several regimes perform equally well in directing a disturbance to least troublesome destinations, all are marked "A." The rankings apply only to a particular disturbance (the table should be read horizontally, one row at a time).

run outcome for financial markets and for the economy is—on *some* occasions—bound to be more adverse than would have been the case under a different operating regime. No one regime can possibly be appropriate for all seasons.

The specific manner in which this conclusion emerges from the schematic framework used here is different in detail from what would emerge from a more complex and realistic framework incorporating additional aspects of the behavior of financial markets and the real sectors of the economy. Nonetheless, the conclusion itself is robust. A more complex framework would show even more convincingly that any one operating regime is bound to be "wrong" some of the time.

Theoretical Arguments and Empirical Evidence Indecisive

Given the dilemma that no one operating regime dominates for all types of disturbance, the Federal Reserve must choose that regime thought likely to prove best on average.

As a starting point for discussion, I consider an extremely simple-minded approach. Suppose the Federal Reserve were, in effect, to count the number of A's and F's in each column of table 3-1—in practice, an analogous table derived from a more realistic model of the entire economy—and award the prize to the regime receiving the largest number of A's or smallest number of F's. No matter how realistic the underlying model, adoption of this approach would be obviously wrong. Such a ranking of the regimes would implicitly assume that the various types of nonpolicy disturbance merit equal weights in the choice of regime. In real life, however, different types of disturbance are not equally important—not in how large they are, how often they occur, nor how long they last.

To illustrate, table 3-1 shows that the funds-rate regime is preferred for all types of disturbance on the supply side of the money market and for changes in money demand due to shifts in asset preferences. The "only" instances in which the funds-rate regime receives the failing grade are those in which money demand changes because of disturbances in the real sectors of the economy that alter aggregate demand. Would it then be sensible to conclude that, on balance, the Federal Reserve should operate with the funds-rate regime?

Patently not. Of all the types of disturbance shown in table 3-1, the last category that includes all disturbances originating outside financial markets may well be the most important. On average, such disturbances may occur more frequently. They may be larger. Moreover, many real-sector disturbances that cause aggregate demand to rise or fall may persist for longer periods. For one or more of these reasons, disturbances originating in the real sectors of the economy may well also be the most harmful type of disturbance (have the greatest potential for adversely affecting the ultimate targets of macroeconomic policy). Even though the funds-rate regime performs poorly only when disturbances originate in the real sectors of the economy, therefore, that one fact may be more than sufficient to remove it from the competition for first prize.[1]

The arguments summarized in the last paragraph are thought by many to establish a strong presumption against use of the funds-rate regime. But that case is presumptive, not conclusive. Suppose, furthermore, that the Federal Reserve decides against the funds-rate regime. On what grounds should it choose among the four quantity regimes?

The total-reserves regime is probably better than any other in handling real-sector disturbances that are transmitted through changes in aggregate demand. And the total-reserves regime induces a benign outcome when unexpected changes occur in discount-window borrowing and in asset preferences for currency. Yet the total-reserves regime fosters the worst outcome when nonbanks shift their asset preferences for deposits and when unexpected changes occur in banks' reserves (excess or required). The unborrowed-reserves regime performs excellently in coping with shifts in asset preferences for currency and performs markedly better than the total-reserves regime in mitigating the adverse consequences of disturbances in excess reserves, in required reserves, and in asset preferences for deposits. However, the unborrowed-reserves regime permits the worst outcome for unexpected changes in discount-window borrowing. Among the four quantity regimes, moreover, the unborrowed-reserves regime provides the least resistance to real-sector disturbances. The base and the portfolio regimes have still different combinations of merits and demerits.

1. In this schematic framework the discount rate and the federal funds rate are the only interest rates that appear explicitly; r^{ff} is thus the only interest rate that can adjust to market forces. In a more realistic and complex model that includes several interest rates adjusting to clear market excess demands, a funds-rate operating regime would keep r^{ff} at a predetermined setting but would not prevent other interest rates from changing. Critics of the funds-rate regime are therefore correct in emphasizing that although r^{ff} might be less variable under a funds-rate regime than under other regimes, it does not necessarily follow that *all* interest rates would be less variable.

If the Federal Reserve cannot reasonably choose an operating regime merely by counting the various grades in the columns of a table like table 3-1, it also cannot reasonably use any simple, theoretical rule of thumb for weighting the grades. At a minimum, a sensible choice should depend on empirical evidence about the (average) frequency, size, and duration of the various types of disturbance in the past and a judgment about the likelihood of the past pattern continuing into the future.

Economists at present do not have sufficiently reliable empirical knowledge about the (average) behavior of the U.S. economy to be able, with confidence, to assign relative weights to the various types of disturbance.

As suggested above, there is ample evidence that large unexpected changes in behavior originate from time to time in the goods and labor markets of the economy, and that some of these disturbances persist for several calendar quarters. Accurate, detailed knowledge about the origin and severity of those real-sector disturbances, however, is not available.

It is possible to make some broad generalizations about disturbances originating within the financial markets. For example, unexpected changes in float and in the government's deposit balance are significant in the very short run but they are also transitory. (Data for these variables exhibit day-to-day and week-to-week fluctuations that are large and erratic, whereas monthly and quarterly averages of the series show only modest variation and little or no secular trend.) Unexpected changes in excess reserves can be sizable in the short run, but they too tend to be transitory. To take another illustration: disturbances in nonbanks' demands for deposits have on occasion been both large and persistent, especially in the last decade. Generalizations such as these about disturbances originating in financial markets, however, are also much less firmly grounded in detailed research than is desirable.[2]

Because empirical knowledge is insufficient to permit confident judgments about the relative frequencies, sizes, and durations of prospective disturbances, the Federal Reserve does not have stronger empirical than theoretical grounds for choosing its operating regime for implementing monetary policy.[3]

2. Some suggestive evidence about unexpected changes in deposits, currency, excess reserves, and discount-window borrowing during 1979–82 is presented in chapter 4 below.

3. The insufficiency of empirical knowledge about the origin and severity of nonpolicy disturbances is due primarily to the inherent difficulties of research on this topic. Another contributing factor, however, is the insensitivity of some economists to the need for such empirical knowledge.

Instrument Variation: A Partial Escape

The considerations advanced so far suggest an agnostic approach to the problem of instrument choice. The case for agnosticism is still stronger when one takes into account the point about instrument *variation* mentioned in chapter 2.

Recall that the Federal Reserve, regardless of its choice of operating regime, need not commit itself to predetermined instrument settings except over the very short run. The longest interval for which such a commitment can be described as "required" or "bureaucratically inevitable" is the interval between the periodic meetings of the Federal Open Market Committee (FOMC). Since the FOMC can, and on a number of occasions does, have special telephone meetings in between its regularly scheduled meetings, this interval is at most only one or two weeks long.

For all but the shortest run, therefore, the Federal Reserve can partially escape the dilemma of instrument choice. The partial escape comes from the ability to use discretionary instrument variation as an offset to adverse developments that may arise under the particular operating regime in force at the time.

In the shortest run, of course, the Federal Reserve cannot know with confidence which nonpolicy disturbances may be occurring and hence whether its operating regime is directing the disturbances to benign or troublesome destinations. Information about the current state of the economy, and even about financial markets, is sometimes inaccurate and in any case is incomplete. Once adverse developments have occurred and have been identified, moreover, it may not be feasible or desirable to try to reverse them promptly. The existence of great uncertainty about how the economy works and about how Federal Reserve actions affect the economy makes it dangerous to engage in aggressive instrument manipulation (certainty-equivalent "fine-tuning"). The FOMC, for political or bureaucratic reasons, may prove to be timid in adapting instrument settings to changed circumstances. For all these reasons, the problem of instrument choice is not trivial.

Nonetheless, the either-or choice of operating regimes pales in significance relative to medium- and long-run discretionary decisions about instrument variation. The problem of instrument choice can only become a first-order concern in monetary policy if the Federal Reserve decides, or is statutorily instructed, to eschew discretionary instrument adaptation in favor of simple rules for the time paths of its instrument settings.

Some Further Arguments

For the moment, suppose it is taken for granted that the Federal Reserve discretionarily adapts its instrument settings to new information about the economy and financial markets. According to one school of thought, the choice of operating procedure should then be determined primarily by the performance of alternative regimes in handling short-run, transitory disturbances. Proponents of this view note that unexpected disturbances of any sort cannot be immediately identified by the Federal Reserve when they first occur, and hence cannot be promptly offset by discretionary instrument variation. When a disturbance is both large and persistent, however, the Federal Reserve will in due course be able to identify it and to contemplate offsetting action. According to this view, therefore, the Federal Reserve should seek, in effect, a division of labor between instrument choice and instrument variation. Nonpolicy disturbances tending to occur frequently, to be transitory, and to be especially difficult to identify as they occur should receive proportionately more weight when the operating regime is selected. Conversely, disturbances tending to occur less frequently, to be persistent, and to be less difficult to identify should receive less weight. These latter disturbances should receive less weight in the decision about instrument choice, it is argued, not because they are inherently less troublesome—indeed, the presumption is the contrary—but because persisting disturbances can be more reliably offset with instrument variation.

The argument in the preceding paragraph has considerable merit. But it is vulnerable to several counterarguments.

The first objection is a variant of a point already made. If the preceding approach to instrument choice were adopted, some large and persisting disturbances would in the first instance be directed to troublesome destinations. Desirable "adjustment" of financial variables could thus be delayed relative to the adjustment that would have occurred under an alternative regime. As an illustration, suppose the Federal Reserve adopts the funds-rate regime, relying on the argument that the funds-rate regime does commendably well in handling short-run, transitory disturbances on both the supply and demand sides of the money market. When a large and persistent disturbance originates in the real sectors of the economy, however, the funds-rate regime prevents immediate changes in interest rates. The real-sector shock therefore meets little or no resistance in the financial markets and may be permitted to generate considerable upward or downward momentum in economic activity before the Federal Reserve takes a discretionary decision to raise or lower the federal funds rate.

The second counterargument emphasizes not the delay in the Federal Reserve's ability to identify large and persisting disturbances, but rather the political or sociological inhibitions that may constrain the Federal Reserve from making prompt changes in its instrument settings. The politics of overall macroeconomic policy in the United States, not excluding policy deliberations within the Federal Reserve System, tend to impart an inertia to decisionmaking. Quite apart from the politics, moreover, policymakers confronted with severe uncertainty may often choose to act with excessive hesitancy. Many observers of the Federal Reserve's use of the funds-rate regime in the 1960s and 1970s (including a number of observers inside the Federal Reserve) believe that the monetary authority often failed to adjust the funds rate sufficiently promptly in the face of growing evidence that such action was desirable. If, for political or sociological reasons, the Federal Reserve is prone to vary its policy instruments too sluggishly, the case advanced above for selecting the operating regime to deal with short-run, transitory disturbances and leaving persistent disturbances to be dealt with by discretionary instrument variation is a recipe for trouble.

The last few points raised open up a broad and fundamental issue: to what extent should monetary policy be discretionarily "active"? It is not feasible here to analyze the controversy over rules versus discretion in its several dimensions and complexities. It should be obvious, however, that a complete discussion of the dilemma of instrument choice requires such an analysis.

Concluding Comment

It is tempting to say more about the Federal Reserve's choice of operating regime. (Most of the points summarized in this chapter merit a much more careful analysis than can be included here.) It is also tempting to present, and to try to justify, my own tentative personal view about instrument choice: namely, that the unborrowed-reserves regime may be a reasonable compromise for the Federal Reserve between the more extreme choices of the funds-rate regime and the total-reserves regime. If this book is to be kept within manageable bounds, however, the reader must be content with the preceding summary of arguments about operating regimes, agnostic though it may be.[4]

In the next chapter I turn to the implications of the preceding analysis for the interpretation of variations in the stock of money.

4. On the choice among operating regimes, the relative importance of instrument choice and instrument variation, the appropriate treatment of uncertainty in formulating discretionary policy, the distinction between discretionary instrument adaptation and fine tuning, and the main elements in the rules versus discretion controversy, see Ralph C. Bryant, *Money and Monetary Policy in Interdependent Nations* (Brookings Institution, 1980), chaps. 14–19. Chapters 20–25 of that book integrate the analysis of these issues for both the domestic and the external aspects of monetary policy.

CHAPTER FOUR

Control of the Money Stock in the Short Run

How closely can the Federal Reserve control the money stock? "Closely" presumably implies that deviations in the money stock from specified target values should be minor. Since both the target and the actual money stock are a time series of values, however, "minor" cannot be meaningfully defined in the absence of a temporal reference period. With a very short reference period (say, one or two weeks), a discrepancy between the actual path and the target path of the money stock by as much as X percent of the target path might be thought minor. With a reference period as long as a year, on the other hand, a difference of the same X percent between the *annual averages* of the target and actual paths might be thought much too large to be consistent with close control.

In this and the next two chapters I focus on a relatively short reference period of only two to three months. For brevity, this temporal horizon is labeled the "short run." Chapter 7 discusses control of the money stock over longer periods.

Precise Short-run Control Not Possible

Over the short run, as the analysis in previous chapters makes clear, some sort of nonpolicy factors are virtually certain to influence the money stock under any Federal Reserve operating regime.

If the Federal Reserve uses the total-reserves regime to try to control the money stock, the money stock is pushed up (down) by unexpected declines (increases) in required reserves and in the banks' demand for excess reserves. Unexpected increases (declines) in nonbanks' asset preferences for deposits lead under a total-reserves regime to an unexpected rise (decline) in short-term interest rates and an unexpected fall (rise) in the money stock. Unforeseen cyclical movements in the goods and labor markets of the economy exert a procyclical pull on the money stock even under the total-reserves regime (though to a lesser extent than under any of the other potential operating regimes).

If the Federal Reserve uses the base regime as its operating procedure, the money stock will be pushed up or down by unexpected changes in required reserves, by unexpected shifts in banks' demands for excess reserves, by unexpected shifts in nonbanks' asset preferences for both deposits and currency, and by unexpected shifts in aggregate demand.

If the Federal Reserve uses the funds-rate regime, the money stock is protected from nonpolicy disturbances on the supply side of the money market. Shifts in nonbanks' asset preferences for currency and deposits, however, are routinely accommodated under a funds-rate regime; the Federal Reserve's maintenance of the federal funds rate through open-market operations automatically changes bank reserves in the quantity necessary to permit a dollar-for-dollar response of the money stock to the initiating demand disturbance.[1] As emphasized earlier, moreover, the funds-rate regime—quite undesirably—permits unforeseen disturbances originating in the goods and labor markets of the economy to cause large changes in the money stock (larger than under any other operating regime).

If the unborrowed-reserves regime is used to control money, nonpolicy disturbances tend to generate consequences that are intermediate between the consequences generated under the total-reserves and the funds-rate regimes. The money stock is buffeted by unexpected changes in banks' demands for reserves to a smaller degree under the unborrowed-reserves than under the total-reserves regime; yet unlike under the funds-rate regime, some undesired effects on the money stock do occur. The unborrowed-reserves regime permits larger changes in the money stock than does the total-reserves regime in response to surprise changes in aggregate demand attributable to disturbances originating in the real sectors of the economy; in sharp contrast with the funds-rate regime, however, it does permit some changes in the federal funds rate and other short-term interest rates, thereby helping financial markets to provide some resistance to the disturbances in the real sectors. Among all five

1. Although such changes in the money stock can cause deviations of money from a predetermined target path, recall that this outcome has less troublesome consequences for the Federal Reserve's ultimate-target variables than the consequences that result under other operating regimes.

Figure 4-1. *M1 Definition of the Money Stock: Actual Path and Target Cones, Fall 1979 through Summer 1982*[a]

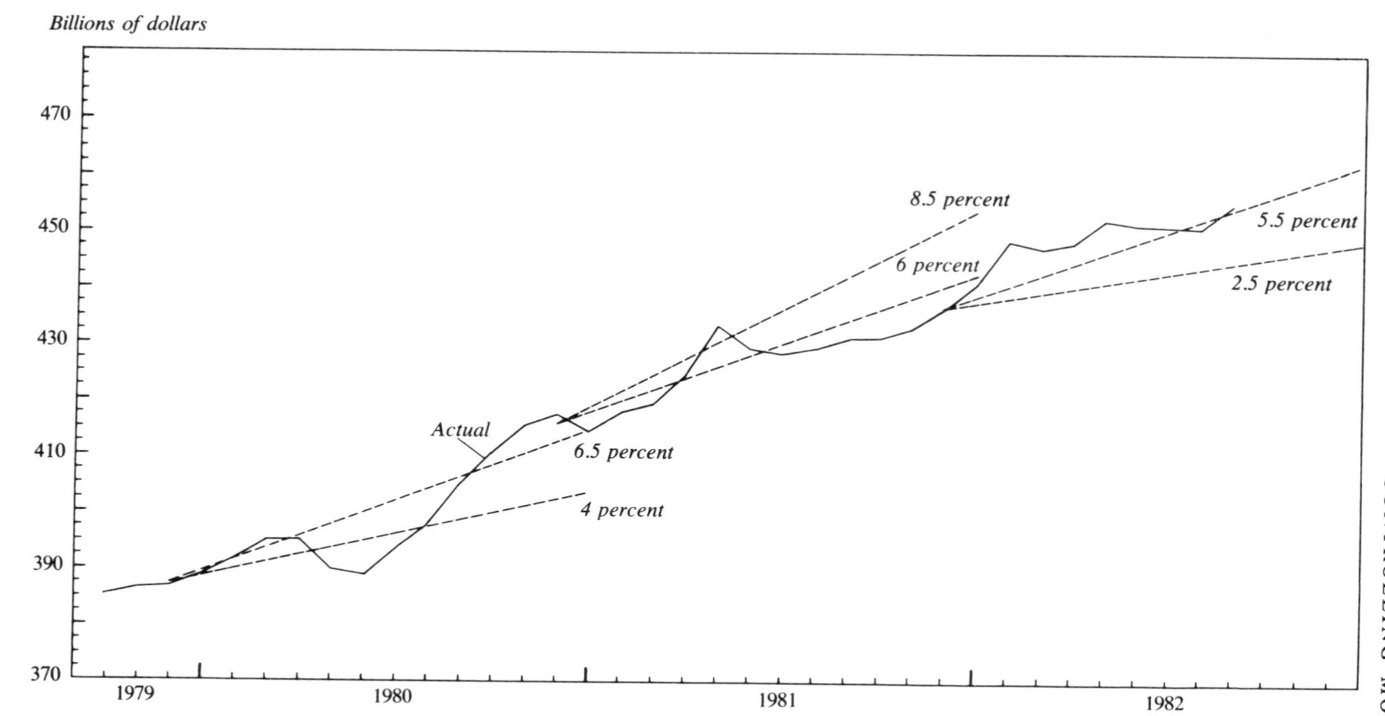

Source: Board of Governors of the Federal Reserve System.
a. Seasonally adjusted monthly averages of daily data.

operating regimes, the unborrowed-reserves regime is least adequate in preventing undesired effects on money and interest rates due to unexpected variations in the banks' demands for borrowing at the Federal Reserve discount window.

If the Federal Reserve decided to use the portfolio regime to try to control money, each type of nonpolicy disturbance analyzed in chapter 2 would have some effect on the money stock and on short-term interest rates. The effects on money from real-sector disturbances would be larger than under the total-reserves regime, but smaller than under the funds-rate regime. Undesired effects on money stemming from unexpected shifts in banks' reserve demands would be handled relatively well under the portfolio regime (better than under any other regime except the funds-rate regime). On the other hand, autonomous shifts in currency demand would be handled relatively poorly. Unlike any of the other four regimes, the portfolio regime would permit the money stock to be pushed up or down by unexpected variations in float and in the government's deposit balance.

The various nonpolicy disturbances identified in this analysis are common in real life. It is highly likely that one or more of them will occur, in sizes large enough to have significant effects, within any short-run period. Over a short run, therefore—certainly within a single month, and almost surely for a period of three months or less—substantial variations in the money stock due to nonpolicy factors are sometimes unavoidable no matter what operating procedure the Federal Reserve may employ. Close control of money over this short horizon, defined as continuous prevention of sizable deviations of the actual stock from a predetermined target path, is just not possible.

Nonpolicy Influences: Some Facts and Inferences, 1979–82

What has been said so far about nonpolicy factors influencing the stock of money can be concretely illustrated from recent experience.

Figure 4-1 shows the monthly averages of the path of the M1 definition of the U.S. money stock between fall 1979 and summer 1982.[2] The points

2. I focus on M1 only because it has received greater attention than other monetary aggregates. M1 (referred to as M1-B in 1980 and 1981) is defined as the sum of currency in circulation, traveler's checks, demand deposits, and other checkable deposits. These same points apply, with some modifications, to the narrower aggregate M1-A (M1 less

Figure 4-2. *M1 Definition of the Money Stock, Weekly Data, Fall 1979 through Summer 1982*[a]

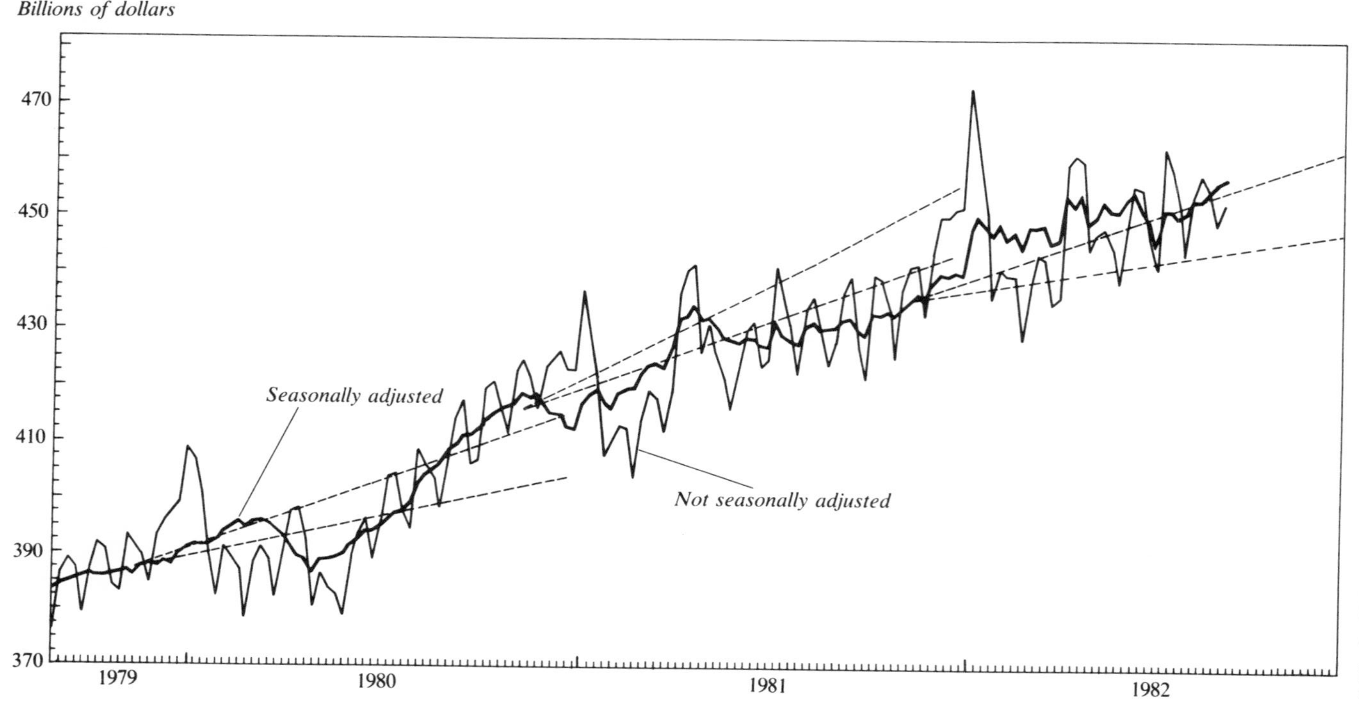

Source: Board of Governors of the Federal Reserve System.
a. Weekly averages of daily data. See figure 4-1 for rates of growth defining the target cones.

plotted in the figure are seasonally adjusted monthly averages of daily data. Figure 4-1 also indicates the target "cones" specified by the Federal Open Market Committee for the twelve-month periods from the fourth quarter to the fourth quarter for 1979–80, 1980–81, and 1981–82.[3]

The growth of M1 over the three-year period from 1980 to 1982 was anything but smooth. That fact is evident even in the monthly average data in figure 4-1. For the same period figure 4-2 shows the data for *weekly* averages of M1, both before and after seasonal adjustment. As can be seen by comparing the two figures, the weekly observations for seasonally adjusted M1 exhibit markedly greater variability than the monthly averages, and the actual data before seasonal adjustment contain very large week-to-week fluctuations that are smoothed out by the seasonal adjustment process.

After a spurt of growth in February 1980 that put the actual level above the target cone, M1 fell sharply in the spring and was well below the target cone until the early summer. From the summer through the fall of 1980, M1 grew rapidly; by November the monthly average of actual M1 was almost 2.5 percent above the midpoint of the target cone. M1 fell sharply in December 1980, surged above the target path in March and April 1981, fell absolutely in May and June to well below the target path, and then grew only sluggishly between early summer and October 1981. During the final weeks of 1981 and early January 1982, growth again became vigorous. Because the Federal Reserve established the target cone for 1982 using as a base the average of actual M1 during the fourth quarter of 1981, the level of M1 by January 1982 was well above the 1982 target cone. M1 remained significantly above the target cone throughout the first five months of 1982. By the latter part of June, three successive weeks of absolute decline had brought M1 back inside the Federal Reserve's target range. As the summer progressed, however, M1 moved back to the top of, and then above, the target cone.

Many observers of financial developments labeled these 1980–82

---

other checkable deposits) and to the broader aggregates M2 and M3. See chapter 9 for figures depicting M2 and M3 analogous to figure 4-1.

3. The target growth range for M1 for 1981 was increased to a range of 6.0 to 8.5 percent from the 1980 range of 4.0 to 6.5 percent to allow for one-time shifts in 1981 into NOW accounts out of deposits not included in M1. On a "shift-adjusted" basis, the 1981 target growth range was *lowered* to 3.5 percent to 6.0 percent. Figure 4-1 plots the 1981 target cone for M1, not for shift-adjusted M1. The data underlying figure 4-1 and the subsequent figures are based on the data available to me as of September 1982. The monetary aggregates data incorporate the benchmark revisions of February 1982.

movements in the money stock "erratic" and interpreted them as evidence that the Federal Reserve was conducting monetary policy badly. Such critics presumed that M1 could have been made to grow much more smoothly, and hence kept well within the target cones, if the Federal Reserve had merely adjusted its actions to achieve this objective.

Some especially prominent examples of this criticism occurred during the first half of 1982. It was then asserted that the prevailing high level of interest rates and the weakness of real activity in the U.S. economy were importantly, or even primarily, attributable to the erratic pattern of money growth in 1980 and 1981. It was further asserted that the Federal Reserve could easily have avoided the erratic pattern of money growth in 1980–81. The failure of money to grow smoothly along a target path was attributed to the Federal Reserve's lack of genuine intent to achieve that result.[4]

Assertions such as these are, at the very least, incomplete and misleading. They de-emphasize or altogether ignore the nonpolicy factors influencing money. What is worse, they undermine a better public understanding of why the economy and financial markets have performed poorly in recent years.

The remainder of this chapter provides some facts and inferences about the nonpolicy factors influencing the money stock in 1979–82. The findings cast strong doubt on the presumption that the short-run fluctuations shown in figure 4-1 can be predominantly attributed to "misconduct" of monetary policy by the Federal Reserve.

Unexpected Shifts in Deposit Demand

The top panel of figure 4-3 depicts the deposit component of M1 (that is, demand deposits and other checkable deposits). This deposit series behaves quite similarly to M1 because it represents roughly 70 percent

4. See, for example, Donald Regan, Testimony before the Joint Economic Committee, January 27, 1982; Kenneth H. Bacon, "Regan Attacks Fed for 'Erratic' Policies, Says They Helped Fuel Recession's Onset," *Wall Street Journal*, January 28, 1982; Donald Regan, Speech to the National Association of Accountants, June 21, 1982 (see *New York Times*, June 22, 1982); Eileen Alt Powell, "Treasury Studies Curbs on Power of Fed on Worry Recovery Is Being Undermined," *Wall Street Journal*, June 21, 1982; Milton Friedman, "Monetary Policy: Theory and Practice," *Journal of Money, Credit and Banking*, vol. 14 (February 1982), pp. 98–118; and Friedman, "The Federal Reserve and Monetary Instability," *Wall Street Journal*, February 1, 1982; and Allan H. Meltzer, "The Results of the Fed's Failed Experiment," *Wall Street Journal*, July 29, 1982.

of the latter and because it grows much more irregularly than the other components of M1 (currency and traveler's checks). The top panel of the figure also shows the amount of deposits predicted by a representative deposits equation (equation B-1 in appendix B). The bottom panel makes clear the difference between the two series in the top panel. This prediction error (or, alternatively, the month-to-month change in the error) can be interpreted as a measure of the unexpected, autonomous shifts in deposit demand analyzed in chapter 2.

The equation used to generate the predicted values and errors in figure 4-3 is a variant of one of the equations in the monthly money-market model used by the staff of the Federal Reserve Board. The equation has defects, as do all estimated equations for this variable (or for demand deposits alone). These defects, however, are not centrally important for this discussion. The equation is probably no more inadequate as a description of deposit demand than others currently available. Had a different equation been used to generate figure 4-3, similar qualitative conclusions would have emerged.

The series plotted in the two panels of figure 4-3 show that the periods during which deposits fell sharply are periods for which the prediction errors are negative, and vice versa for periods of rapid deposit growth. This coincidence of timing establishes a presumption that shifts in deposit demand not attributable to ordinary responses to changes in output, prices, and interest rates played an important role in the short-run fluctuations of deposits (and hence M1) during 1979–82.

As an illustration, consider the episode in the spring of 1980 that caused widespread criticism of the Federal Reserve. The data underlying figure 4-3 are as follows (billions of dollars):

	Deposits		*Change in prediction error*
	Actual change	*Predicted change*	
February	2.5	1.6	0.9
March	−0.8	1.9	−2.7
April	−5.8	−1.0	−4.8
May	−1.7	−3.9	2.2
June	3.8	−0.5	4.3

The change in deposits predicted by the equation through March was sharply positive. Even for April, deposits were predicted to fall by only $1 billion. Yet actual deposits already fell $800 million in March and

Figure 4-3. *Deposit Component of M1: Actual, Predicted, and Prediction Error, October 1979 through June 1982*[a]

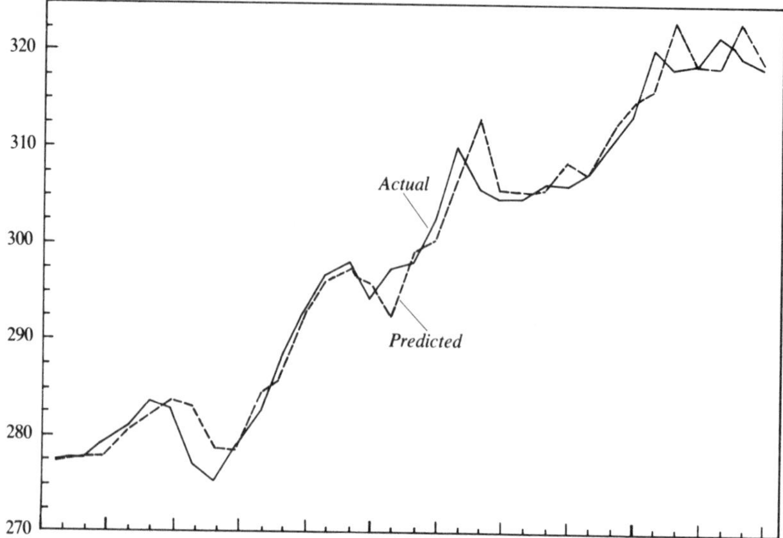

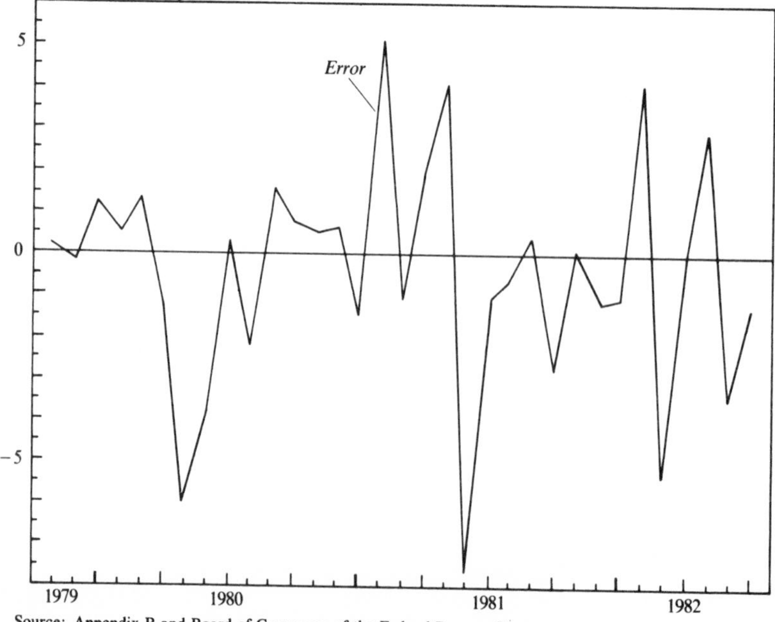

Source: Appendix B and Board of Governors of the Federal Reserve System.

a. Seasonally adjusted monthly averages of daily data. Equation B-1 in appendix B was used to generate the predicted series.

were down by almost $6 billion in April. The level of deposits in May continued to be well below the predicted level even though predicted deposits were finally falling sharply. Neither the Federal Reserve nor anyone else expected the extent of the deposit weakness that developed in late March and in April and May, not even those who were most alert to the possible consequences of the special package of policy measures announced by President Carter on March 14. The consequences for interest rates and the money stock of the unexpected weakness in deposits correspond broadly to those identified in the schematic analysis above.[5]

During several subsequent subperiods in 1980–82 the deposit component of the money stock again changed by large amounts not readily attributable to changes in the economic variables customarily included in equations representing money demand. The surge in March–April 1981, the sluggish growth between early summer and early fall of 1981, and the very large increases in the last weeks of 1981 and early weeks of 1982 are all examples of such unexpected shifts in deposit demand.[6]

For the period shown in figure 4-3 the average of the absolute values of the monthly changes in deposits was $2.7 billion. If the absolute values of the changes in prediction errors are averaged for the period, the figure is $3.2 billion. In many months, the change in the unpredictable component of deposit demand was substantially larger than the change in deposits itself!

In the past few years many researchers have examined the problem

5. For an account of this episode from the perspective of the trading desk at the Federal Reserve Bank of New York, see Peter D. Sternlight and others, "Monetary Policy and Open Market Operations in 1980," *Federal Reserve Bank of New York Quarterly Review*, vol. 6 (Summer 1981), pp. 70–72. The equation used to generate the predicted series for M1 in figure 4-3 contains a term correcting for autocorrelation in the residuals. Such a correction helps to keep the predicted series close to the actual series—with a one-month lag—even when the explanatory variables in the basic equation fail to predict major changes in M1. See appendix B for further discussion. In the absence of the mechanical correction for autocorrelation in the residuals, the predicted series would exhibit much less of a decline in May–June 1980 than that shown in figure 4-3.

6. The autocorrelation correction in the equation used to generate the predicted series in figure 4-3 again plays a key role in helping the predicted series track the actual series even though the basic equation itself inadequately captures the fluctuations in deposit demand. For example, significant parts (though not all) of the increases for the predicted series in May 1981, February 1982, and May 1982 are attributable to this mechanical correction for the failure of the equation in the immediately preceding months (in, respectively, April 1981, January 1982, and April 1982).

Figure 4-4. *Currency Component of M1: Actual, Predicted, and Prediction Error, October 1979 through June 1982*[a]

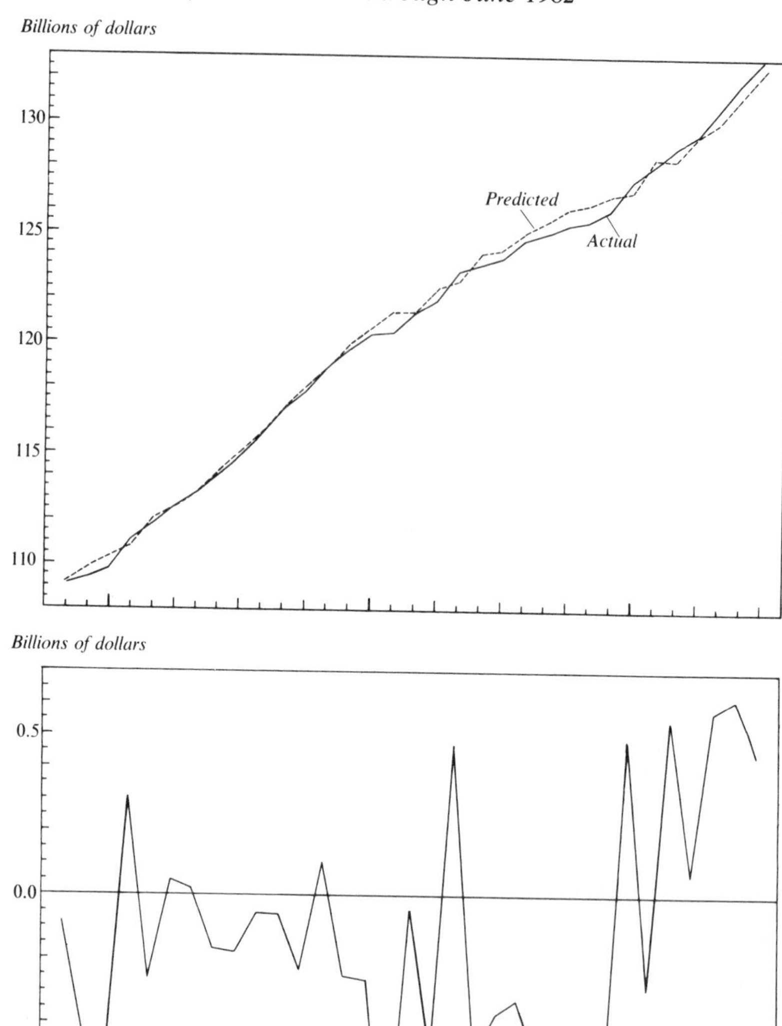

Source: Appendix B and Board of Governors of the Federal Reserve System.

a. Seasonally adjusted monthly averages of daily data. Equation B-2 in appendix B was used to generate the predicted series.

of unexpected shifts in deposit demand. Relevant studies include those by Goldfeld, by Tinsley and Garrett, by Simpson and Porter, and by members of the staff of the Federal Reserve Board in the 1981 staff study of the new operating procedures (see appendix B). This recent literature on money demand tells a story qualitatively the same as that summarized in figure 4-3.

Research will continue trying to gain a better understanding of the behavior of various types of deposits in the U.S. financial system. It may eventually prove possible to identify more reliable demand equations. In the meantime, the burden of the evidence is strongly on the side of the presumptions that deposit demand is occasionally subject to large, unexplained shifts and that these shifts cause substantial fluctuations in actual deposits and actual M1.

Unexpected Shifts in Currency Demand

Figure 4-4 presents actual, predicted, and error series for the nondeposit component of M1 analogous to the series for deposits in figure 4-3. The nondeposit component is primarily currency in circulation outside banks, although it also includes a small amount of traveler's checks ($3.7 billion in September 1979).

The equation used to generate the predicted and error series in figure 4-4 is described in appendix B. It is a variant of the equation for currency plus traveler's checks in the monthly money-market model of the Federal Reserve Board staff and is again representative of the least inadequate equations estimated by other researchers.

As can be readily seen in figure 4-4, currency growth is considerably less irregular than the growth in deposits. And prediction errors for currency demand are markedly smaller in absolute size than those for deposits. There is no doubt, therefore, that deposit demand is a more important source of troublesome disturbances than currency demand.

Unexpected changes in currency holdings, however, are not trivially small. Beginning in late 1980, for example, actual currency growth was weaker than that predicted by the currency equation for five consecutive months; the shortfall was more than $900 million in January 1981. Then in April 1981 the prediction error turned positive by almost $500 million. This movement in April coincided with a large positive error in deposits demand (see figure 4-3); both errors contributed to the April 1981 surge in M1 (figure 4-1). Between May and November 1981, a pronounced

Figure 4-5. *Excess Reserves, Weekly Data, Spring 1979 through Summer 1982*[a]

Millions of dollars

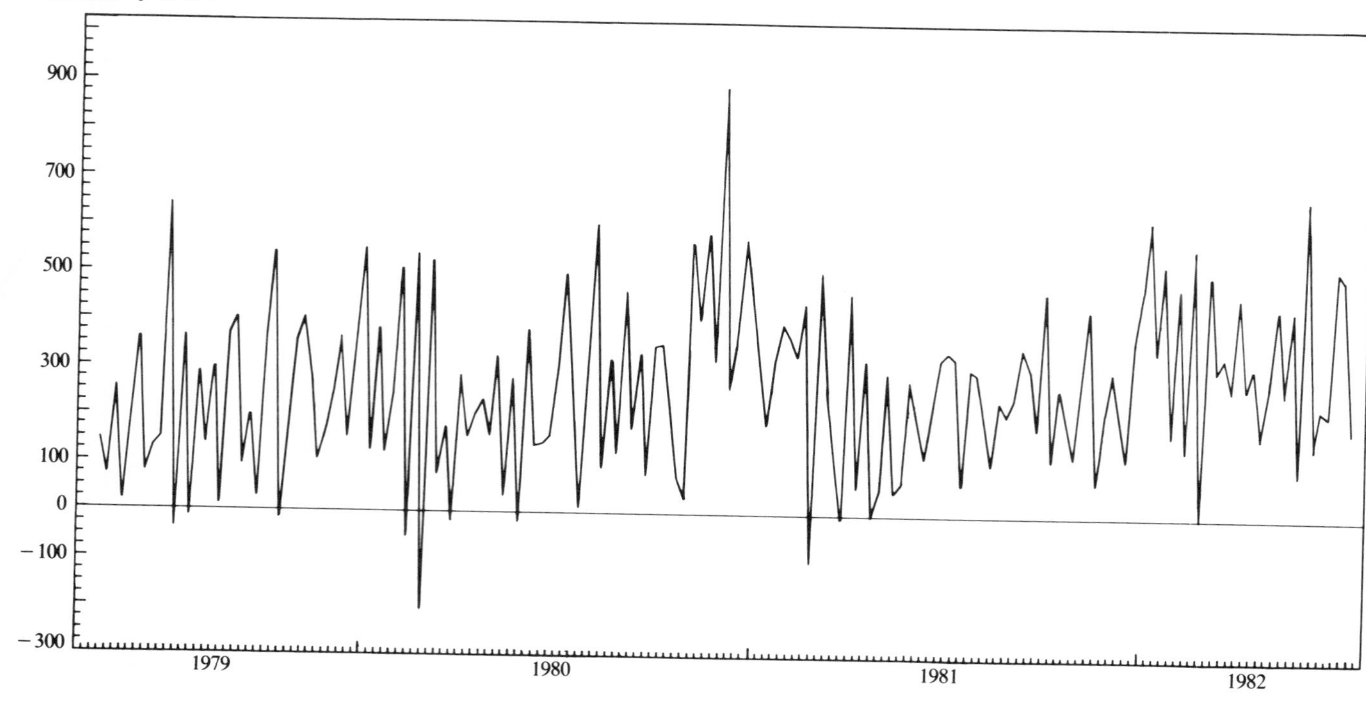

Source: Board of Governors of the Federal Reserve System.

a. Weekly averages of daily data, not seasonally adjusted.

weakness in currency demand relative to expected growth contributed to the sluggishness in growth of M1. In the first half of 1982, currency grew more vigorously than predicted by a representative currency equation, thereby again contributing to the deviation of M1 from the target cone set by the Federal Reserve.

To appraise the significance of unpredicted movements in currency, it is also relevant to note that the typical growth in actual currency holdings is on the order of $650–700 million a month. If this average change is used as a benchmark, first differences in the prediction error like those between March and May 1981 (an increase in April of $980 million followed by a decrease in May of $980 million) or those between December 1981 and February 1982 (an increase of $1,110 million, a decrease of $790 million, and an increase of $835 million) scarcely seem trivial.

Unexpected Changes in Excess Reserves

Figure 4-5 presents weekly data for excess reserves from early May 1979 through mid-July 1982. From the infrequent statements about excess reserves made in newspapers or journal articles, one could form the impression that variations in excess reserves are negligible. Figure 4-5 shows, however, that the facts are otherwise. The mean level of excess reserves for the period was only $265 million. But the average of the absolute values of the weekly *changes* was $222 million. As the figure indicates, weekly fluctuations of $500 million or more have occurred on numerous occasions.

If one examines monthly averages of the data, the variance in the series is much smaller. But it is still not trivial, as can be seen in figure 4-6. (The personnel charged with day-to-day implementation of policy at the Federal Reserve Bank of New York confront the fluctuations in excess reserves as they occur and must decide whether or not to respond mainly on the basis of the weekly fluctuations, not the monthly averages.)

Beginning in September 1968, at the same time lagged reserve accounting was introduced (see chapter 6), the Federal Reserve permitted banks to carry forward for one week a part or all of their current period's surplus or deficiency of required reserves provided that the portion carried over did not exceed 2 percent of their required reserves. Banks could not run deficiencies for two weeks in a row without incurring a penalty; any surplus carried over from the preceding period not used in

Figure 4-6. *Excess Reserves: Actual, Predicted, and Prediction Error, October 1979 through June 1982*[a]

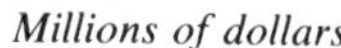

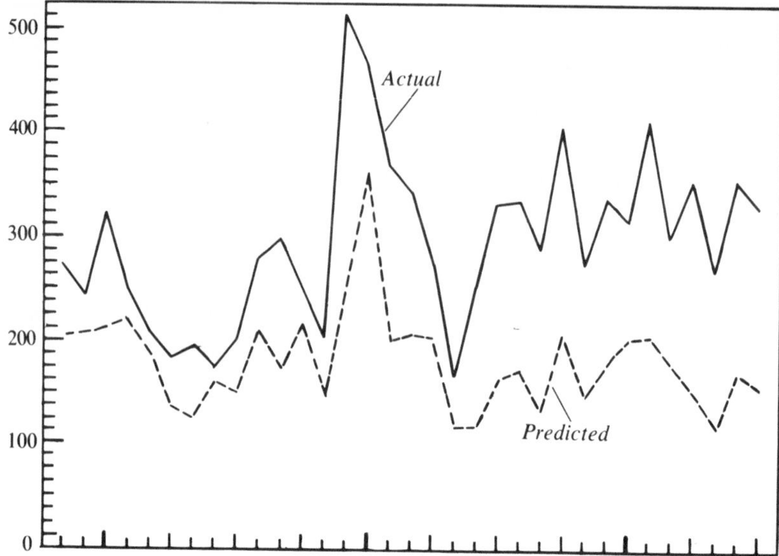

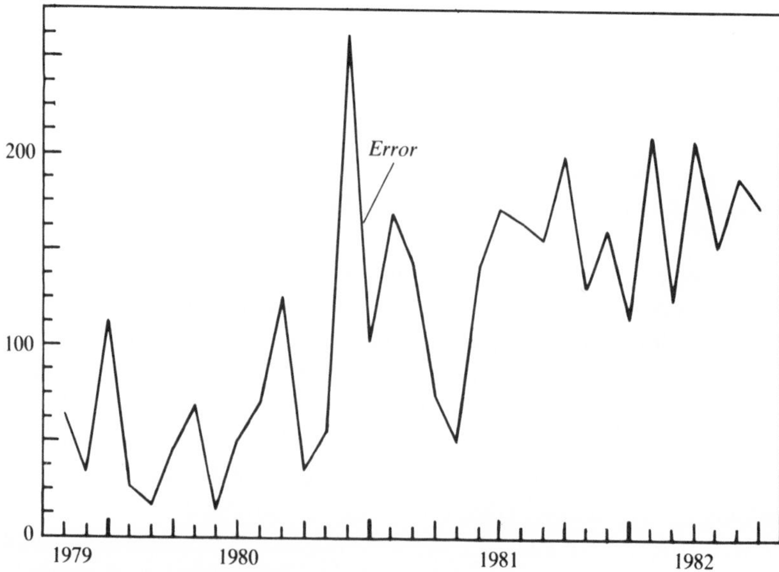

Source: Appendix B and Board of Governors of the Federal Reserve System.

a. Monthly averages of daily data, not seasonally adjusted. Equation B-3 in appendix B was used to generate the predicted series.

the current period was lost. These carry-over privileges have been an important contributing factor to the sharp sawtooth pattern characteristic of the weekly series but much less characteristic of the monthly averages.[7]

The banks' demand for excess reserves is negatively related to the federal funds rate. The size of this interest sensitivity is interrelated with the use being made of the carry-over privileges. This and other aspects of an equation for predicting excess reserves are discussed in appendix B.

Figure 4-6 is constructed in the same manner as figures 4-3 and 4-4. Again, the prediction error plotted in the bottom panel provides a presumptive measure of unexpected disturbances.

Two features of figure 4-6 are especially noteworthy. First, November 1980 through February 1981 is characterized by an unusually large disturbance. A general explanation of this prediction error is readily available. Implementation of the new reserve requirements under the Monetary Control Act began in November 1980. These changes resulted in a large net decline in required reserves (about $2.9 billion). Many additional financial intermediaries were required to maintain reserves under the new law, however, and the large increase in excess reserves in November and December 1980 could have resulted from lack of familiarity with the new reporting requirements, especially by smaller institutions.[8]

Knowing in general that an unusual increase in excess reserves may take place, or is taking place, as a result of statutory changes is not the same as having confidence in how large the increase may be or how long it may persist. The presumption is that the Federal Reserve was uncertain whether to respond to the disturbance in November and December 1980 as it emerged, and if so by how much.[9] Some of the seasonally adjusted

7. For further discussion of the carry-over privileges and of other aspects of variations in excess reserves, see David C. Beek, "Excess Reserves and Reserve Targeting," *Federal Reserve Bank of New York Quarterly Review*, vol. 6 (Autumn 1981), pp. 15–22. In the summer of 1982 the Federal Reserve Board approved in principle a change from lagged reserve accounting to a variant of contemporaneous reserve accounting. As part of this change, the carry-over privileges are to be liberalized.

8. See Beek, "Excess Reserves and Reserve Targeting," p. 18, who also notes that most of the abnormal increase in excess reserves occurred at banks outside New York City.

9. Sternlight and others, "Monetary Policy and Open Market Operations in 1980," pp. 74–75, remark that "excess reserves turned out to be very high in that first week [of implementation of the Monetary Control Act]. In subsequent weeks (through early

Figure 4-7. *Discount-Window Borrowing, Weekly Data, Spring 1979 through Summer 1982*[a]

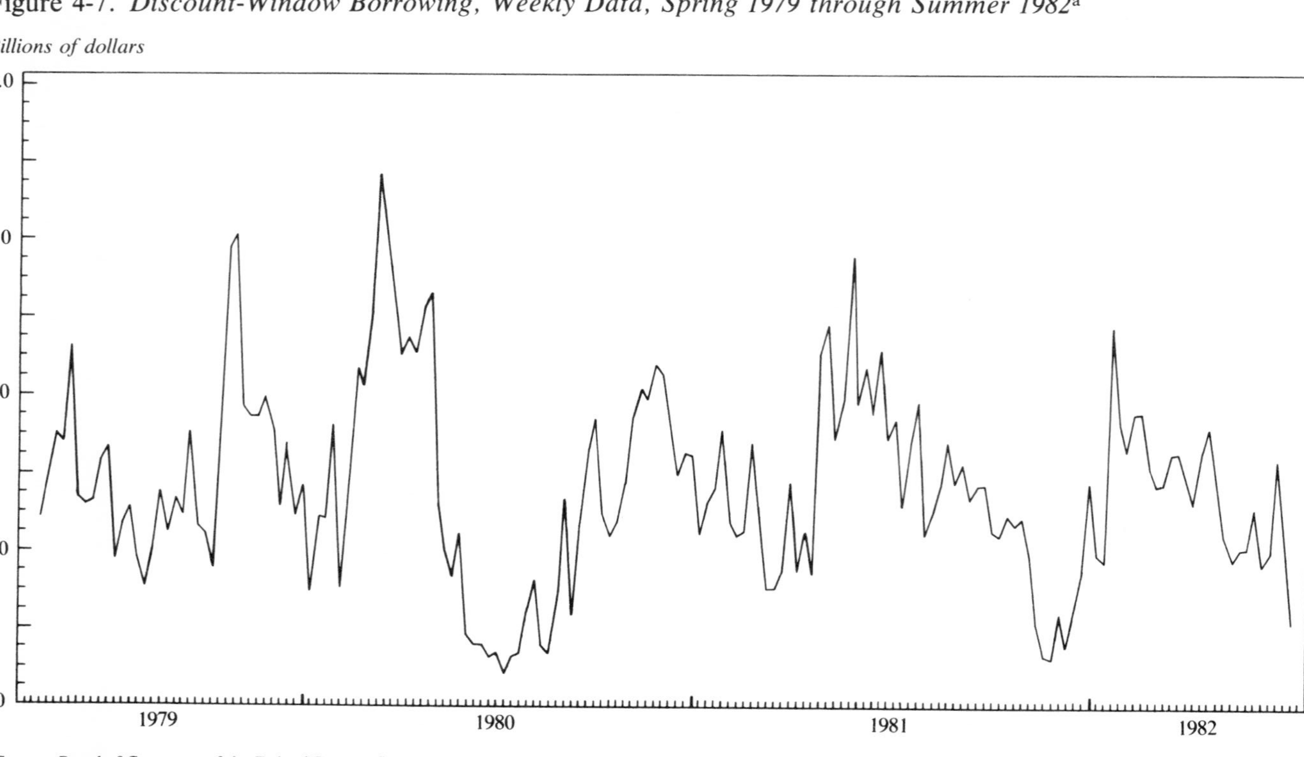

Source: Board of Governors of the Federal Reserve System.
a. Weekly averages of daily data, not seasonally adjusted.

decline in M1 in December 1980 (see figure 4-1) is probably attributable to the unexpectedly high level of excess reserves at that time.

A second noteworthy feature of figure 4-6 is the consistently positive prediction error. For the entire period from October 1979 through June 1982, actual excess reserves turned out to be larger than the values predicted by a least inadequate equation. This underprediction may be partly attributable to the Federal Reserve's change in operating procedures in October 1979, although other inferences are also possible.

Here as in the preceding cases the conclusion that merits emphasis is a simple, negative one. Unexpected variations in excess reserves can be a disruptive nonpolicy influence on interest rates and the money stock. For periods as long as six months or a year, it is true, such variations are largely transitory. But they are far from negligible for a shorter horizon.

Unexpected Changes in Discount-Window Borrowing

Figure 4-7 shows weekly data for borrowing at the Federal Reserve discount window from early May 1979 through mid-July 1982. A comparison with the weekly data for excess reserves in figure 4-5 indicates that borrowing tends to be much larger in absolute size and to vary by larger absolute amounts. (Weekly changes in borrowing in this period were as large as a $1,520 million increase and a $1,330 million reduction. The average of the absolute values of the weekly changes was $333 million.)

Substantial evidence exists showing that the borrowing behavior of the banks is sensitive to the spread between the federal funds rate and the Federal Reserve's discount rate. It is difficult, however, to estimate econometrically a relation linking borrowing, interest rates, and other variables that is plausible and stable. Appendix B reports several equations for monthly averages of borrowing based on a specification developed by Peter Tinsley and his colleagues on the Federal Reserve Board staff. This way of representing the borrowing behavior of the banks seems less inadequate than any other so far put forward. One of these equations (B-5) was used to generate the predicted values and the errors charted in figure 4-8.[10]

1981), excess reserves remained high by historical standards, a development that proved to be puzzling."

10. The data in figure 4-8 exclude "extended-credit" borrowing in the period from August 1981 through June 1982 (see appendix B).

Figure 4-8. *Discount-Window Borrowing: Actual, Predicted, and Prediction Error, October 1979 through June 1982*[a]

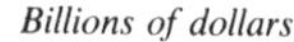

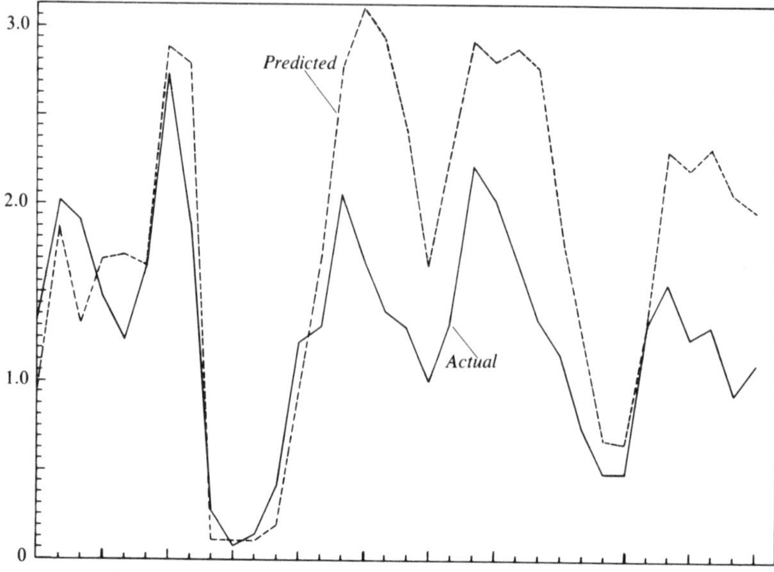

Billions of dollars

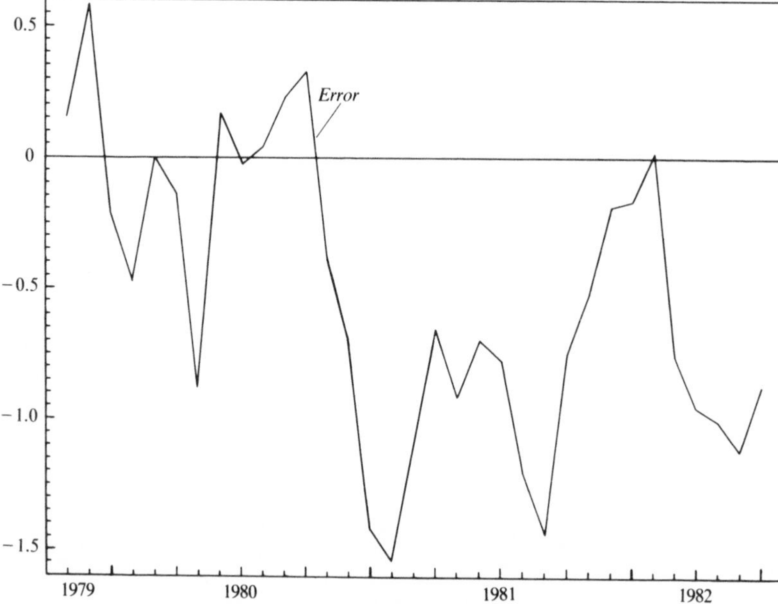

Source: Appendix B and Board of Governors of the Federal Reserve System.

a. Monthly averages of daily data, not seasonally adjusted. Equation B-4 in appendix B was used to generate the predicted series.

For the period shown in figure 4-8, actual borrowing sometimes diverged by large amounts from the predicted series. Especially large errors occurred in April 1980, in December 1980 and January 1981, in July and August 1981, and in the second quarter of 1982.

It seems plausible that the weakness in actual relative to predicted borrowing was a significant factor in holding down M1 in the early winter of 1980–81, and again in the summer of 1981 and the spring of 1982. On the other hand, the unexpected weakness of borrowing in April 1980 cannot have been the primary explanation for the decline of M1 in the spring of 1980. Other things being equal, an unexpected decrease in borrowing puts downward pressure on the money stock (under the unborrowed-reserves operating regime) by *raising* the funds rate and other short-term interest rates. In April and May 1980, the funds rate was falling rapidly. Such a combination of declines in interest rates and in money is characteristic of an unexpected downward shift in asset preferences for deposits (already pointed out in figure 4-3), a sharp decrease in the expansion of aggregate demand (also happening in April and May 1980), or both. Although borrowing behavior was undoubtedly an additional factor complicating monetary policy in the spring of 1980, therefore, other disturbances were more important quantitatively.

After fall 1980 the series for predicted borrowing in figure 4-8 consistently overshoots the actual level. One possible explanation for this phenomenon (and for the large negative error in April 1980) is the penalty surcharge applied to large banks that were frequent borrowers. This surcharge was first instituted in March 1980 as part of the Federal Reserve measures accompanying President Carter's policy recommendations; it was removed after only a few weeks in May 1980. In November 1980, however, it was applied again and kept in force for most of 1981. The predicted series in figure 4-8 does not include the effects of the surcharge, and it thus seems plausible that the overprediction in 1981 is partly attributable to this omission. The continuation of an overprediction in the first half of 1982, on the other hand, cannot be explained in this way; the surcharge was not in force from November 1981 through June 1982.

Because of the equation's inability to deal with the 1980–81 surcharge and for still other reasons mentioned in appendix B, one cannot place great confidence in the equation underlying the predicted and error series in figure 4-8. But that fact only underscores the point emphasized here. Although the Federal Reserve and other analysts of borrowing have *some* basis for predicting how banks will use the discount window, there exists a substantial and highly variable component of borrowing that is not predictable. Such nonpolicy disturbances in turn can have significant effects on short-term interest rates and the money stock.

Atypically Large Disturbances in 1980–82

The errors shown in figures 4-3, 4-4, 4-6, and 4-8 tend to be somewhat larger than similarly calculated errors for years before 1979–82. The inference suggested by this fact is that nonpolicy disturbances in the past several years have been unusually troublesome for the conduct of monetary policy. This inference is developed more systematically and shown to be correct for the period from October 1979 through early 1981 in an analysis by Tinsley, von zur Muehlen, Trepeta, and Fries.[11]

When nonpolicy disturbances are larger or more frequent, *any* Federal Reserve operating procedure will encounter greater difficulties in keeping the money stock close to a target path. Hence the natural interpretation of the experience in 1979–82 is to ascribe a major part of the week-to-week and month-to-month irregularity in the money stock to nonpolicy factors beyond the control of the Federal Reserve rather than to avoidable mistakes in the conduct of policy.

Caveats

The inferences about 1979–82 made above are based on an inspection of the errors from individual econometric equations, with each of several equations examined sequentially. Those inferences can be criticized, with some justification, along two lines.

First, an equation-by-equation examination is less revealing than a systematic empirical analysis of an entire, integrated model. Simulations of an internally consistent model can take into account covariances among disturbances across equations and can therefore modify the inferences derived from analysis of the errors in individual equations.

11. See Peter A. Tinsley and others, "Money Market Impacts of Alternative Operating Procedures," in Board of Governors of the Federal Reserve System, *New Monetary Control Procedures,* vol. 2 (February 1981). See also the insightful review of 1979–81 in David E. Lindsey, "Nonborrowed Reserve Targeting and Monetary Control," in Lawrence Meyer, ed., *Improving Money Stock Control: Problems, Solutions, and Consequences* (Federal Reserve Bank of St. Louis, 1982).

In principle, I would have preferred to work with an integrated model (one incorporating at least all of the money-market relations discussed in appendix A, with both current and lagged responses modeled explicitly). To do so in practice, however, I would have first had to invest a substantial additional amount of time and money in making such a model operational on the Brookings computer. All things considered, an investment of the required magnitude seemed unwarranted. Some entire-model simulations of the preferred sort have already been carried out. The general inferences I have made here are consistent with, and certainly not contradicted by, that evidence.[12]

The second line of criticism stresses the shakiness of the econometric equations underlying any empirical analysis of the sort presented here. One cannot validly identify "errors" or "unexpected disturbances" in a behavioral relation unless some part of the relation—a "predictable" or "expected" component—can be specified with reasonable accuracy. One who takes an extremely skeptical view of the equations presented in appendix B, therefore, will also be agnostic about any inferences based on them.[13]

As already noted, I do not have great confidence in the econometric equations underlying the preceding analysis. But I do believe that the

12. See Tinsley and others, "Money Market Impacts of Alternative Operating Procedures"; and David Lindsey and others, "Monetary Control Experience Under the New Operating Procedures," in the Board, *New Monetary Control Procedures*.

13. This line of criticism can apply both to individual equations and to entire models. For an illustration of a highly agnostic perspective, see Thomas F. Cooley and Stephen F. LeRoy, "Identification and Estimation of Money Demand," *American Economic Review*, vol. 71 (December 1981), pp. 825–44. Cooley and LeRoy deny, in effect, that the economics profession has been able to identify a structural equation for the "demand for money," even to a first approximation. They thus would deny that research is able to identify "unexpected shifts" accurately, even ex post.

Much of econometric research still relies on specifications that treat coefficients as fixed parameters. That assumption is probably invalid in many circumstances. For two recent papers relevant to the subject of this chapter that relax that assumption, see P. A. V. B. Swamy, P. A. Tinsley, and G. R. Moore, "An Autopsy of a Conventional Macroeconomic Relation: The Case of Money Demand," Special Studies Paper 167 (Federal Reserve System, Division of Research and Statistics, April 1982); and D. H. Resler, J. R. Barth, P. A. V. B. Swamy, and W. D. Davis, "Detecting and Estimating Changing Economic Relationships: The Case of Discount Window Borrowings," Special Studies Paper 165 (Federal Reserve Board, Division of Research and Statistics, August 1982). These papers employ the "Swamsley" estimation technique, which is described in P. A. V. B. Swamy and P. A. Tinsley, "Linear Prediction and Estimation Methods for Regression Models with Stationary Stochastic Coefficients," *Journal of Econometrics*, vol. 12, pp. 103–42.

equations can, when cautiously used, contribute to the making of valid inferences.

Note that the caveats just mentioned do not undermine the general conclusion stressed in this chapter. Indeed, the more agnostic one is about economists' empirical knowledge of behavioral relations, the greater the force of the conclusion that unpredictable shifts in the behavior of the private sector can cause sizable week-to-week and month-to-month variations in the money stock.

CHAPTER FIVE

Are Short-run Changes in the Money Multiplier "Small"?

THE MISTAKEN BELIEF that the Federal Reserve can achieve continuous close control over money in successive short-run periods is apparently fostered by an impression that variations in the "multiplier" linking the money stock to the Federal Reserve balance sheet are relatively small and easily predictable.[1] But this impression will not stand up to scrutiny.

One way to grasp the importance of variations in the money multiplier is to decompose the short-run change in money into two components, one part attributable to changes in the multiplier and the other to changes in the reserves supplied by the Federal Reserve. More specifically, let M represent the money stock, H the quantity of reserves (referred to as "high-powered money" in the literature), and k the multiplier linking them. The multiplier is defined as

$$k \equiv M/H. \tag{5-1}$$

For any period, the change in money, ΔM, can be written as the sum of three components in an identity:

$$\Delta M \equiv H_{-1}(\Delta k) + k_{-1}(\Delta H) + (\Delta k)(\Delta H), \tag{5-2}$$

where H_{-1} and k_{-1} are, respectively, the outstanding stock of reserves and the value of the multiplier in the preceding period. The first term, $H_{-1}(\Delta k)$, can be interpreted as the change in M that would occur if the Federal Reserve maintained H unchanged from its value during the previous period. The second term can be interpreted as the change in M

1. For a summary of multiplier approaches to the money supply process, including references to the literature, see Ralph C. Bryant, *Money and Monetary Policy in Interdependent Nations* (Brookings Institution, 1980), pp. 58–60.

Table 5-1. *Decomposition of Changes in M1 with Adjusted Unborrowed Reserves as "High-Powered Money," September 1979 through June 1982*[a]

Billions of dollars

Year and month	Change in money (sum of columns 2 and 3) (1)	Attributable to changes in the multiplier (2)	Attributable to changes in high-powered money (3)
1979			
September	2.1	2.3	−0.2
October	1.2	2.5	−1.3
November	0.4	−2.0	2.4
December	2.1	−8.2	10.3
1980			
January	2.9	−1.6	4.5
February	3.2	10.2	−7.0
March	0.0	13.1	−13.1
April	−5.2	−10.2	5.0
May	−0.9	−15.8	14.9
June	4.7	−2.0	6.7
July	4.3	2.8	1.5
August	7.1	5.0	2.1
September	5.6	5.3	0.3
October	4.8	2.7	2.1
November	2.0	−2.5	4.5
December	−3.0	−7.1	4.1
1981			
January	3.4	1.3	2.1
February	1.5	0.0	1.5
March	5.0	0.3	4.7
April	8.9	10.8	−1.9
May	−4.1	3.6	−7.7
June	−0.8	−2.9	2.1
July	1.0	−4.3	5.3
August	1.7	−2.1	3.8
September	0.1	−5.1	5.2
October	1.7	0.8	0.9
November	3.5	−2.6	6.1
December	4.5	0.0	4.5
1982			
January	7.7	9.2	−1.5
February	−1.3	5.8	−7.1
March	1.0	−3.5	4.5
April	4.0	3.1	0.9
May	−0.8	−7.5	6.7
June	−0.5	−1.0	0.5

Source: Board of Governors of the Federal Reserve System; see the text for an explanation of the calculations.

a. Data are seasonally adjusted monthly averages of daily data available as of July 1982 (after the February 1982 benchmark revisions of the data for the monetary aggregates but before the September 1982 revisions of the data for the reserve aggregates). Money is the M1 definition of the money stock; that is, the sum of currency in circulation, traveler's checks, demand deposits, and other checkable deposits. High-powered money, for the purposes of this table, is defined as the amount of unborrowed reserves adjusted by the staff of the Federal Reserve Board for changes in reserve requirements. The multiplier here is the ratio of M1 to adjusted unborrowed reserves.

that would result from a change in H given an unchanged multiplier. The third, cross-product term is usually small.

If the cross-product term in 5-2 is combined with the second term, the identity is

(5-2a) $$\Delta M \equiv H_{-1}(\Delta k) + k(\Delta H).$$

To divide the change in money into the two components shown in 5-2a is, if anything, to load the case in favor of the view that Federal Reserve actions rather than changes in the multiplier are the primary determinant of changes in money.

Table 5-1 presents the results of calculating 5-2a for September 1979 through June 1982, using the M1 definition for the money stock and adjusted unborrowed reserves as the measure of H. Unborrowed reserves adjusted for changes in reserve requirements is the closest possible approximation to "the" quantity used by the Federal Reserve as its primary instrument during the period following October 1979.

The figures in column 2 of the table are the changes in money attributable to the changes in the multiplier—that is, $H_{-1}(\Delta k)$. Those figures, especially when compared with the actual changes in money in column 1, ought to astonish anyone holding the view that short-run changes in the multiplier are "small." The plain fact is that changes attributable to variations in the multiplier tend very often to be much larger than the actual change in money itself!

The data in table 5-1 are plotted in figure 5-1. Casual inspection of that figure reveals another striking feature of the data. Large short-run changes in the multiplier typically coincide with short-run movements of unborrowed reserves in the opposite direction. Typically, therefore, the two types of changes have *offsetting* effects on the money stock. Causal interpretation of this negative correlation is not straightforward: it is plausible to believe that private decisionmakers in the financial markets react in an offsetting way to Federal Reserve actions and that the Federal Reserve tries to offset nonpolicy disturbances originating in the economy. For the purposes of the simple point under discussion here, however, the direction of causation is not central to the argument. The mere existence of the strong negative correlation undermines the presumption that short-run changes in the multiplier are small in importance relative to the policy actions of the Federal Reserve.[2]

2. The conclusion in the text *could* be incorrect if short-term variations in the multiplier were entirely or predominantly attributable to Federal Reserve operating

Figure 5-1. *Decomposition of Changes in M1 with Adjusted Unborrowed Reserves as "High-Powered Money," June 1979 through June 1982*

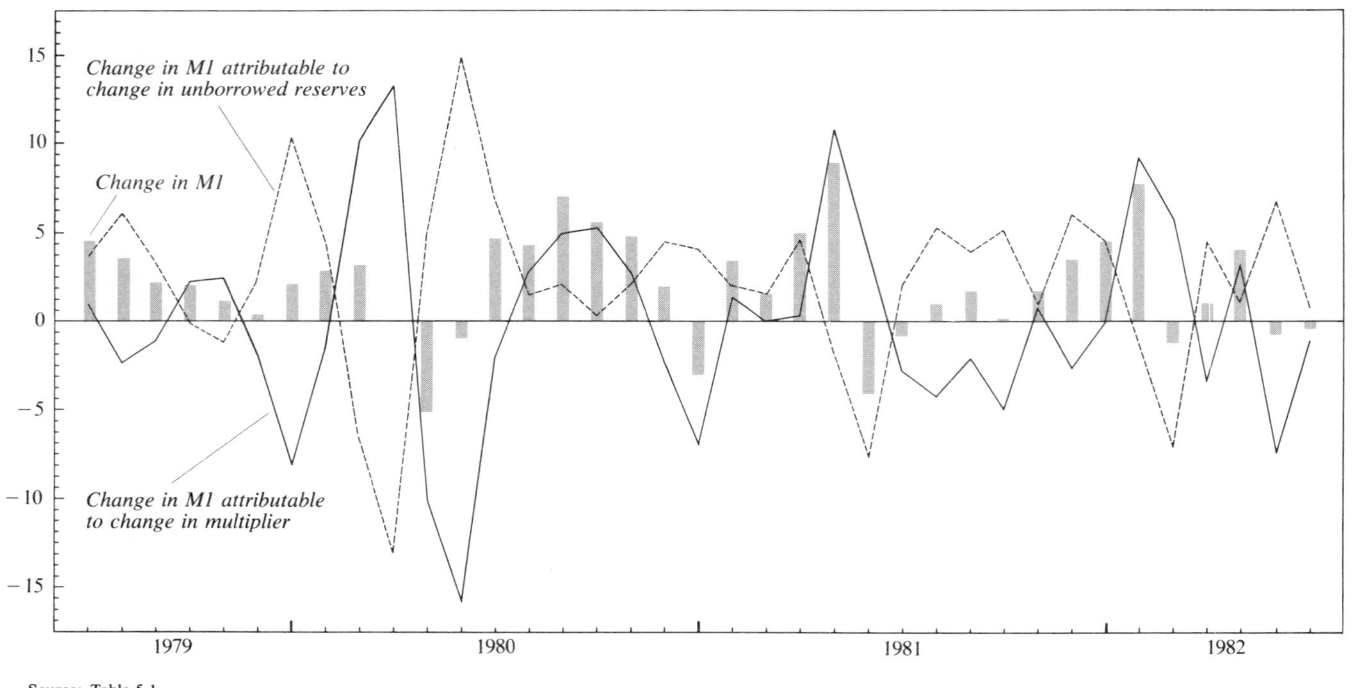

Source: Table 5-1.

Figure 5-2 shows the value of the unborrowed-reserves multiplier in two different ways. The dashed line is the multiplier used in calculating the data in table 5-1 (with unborrowed reserves adjusted for seasonality and for changes in reserve requirements). The solid line shows the multiplier when the data for unborrowed reserves are not adjusted for seasonality or for changes in reserve requirements. It is this latter multiplier, if any, that the Federal Reserve must deal with on a week-to-week basis.[3]

It is sometimes argued that the multiplier linking the monetary base to the money stock is less variable and more predictable than the multipliers for unborrowed reserves or total reserves and is therefore a reliable fulcrum for use in controlling the money stock. This position is argued, for example, by James Johannes and Robert Rasche and by Anatol Balbach.[4] And one frequently encounters charts of the multiplier for the monetary base that give a visual impression that its variability is small.[5]

Yet such assertions and impressions are seriously misleading. Because the monetary base is the sum of currency and reserves and because currency is a magnitude several times larger than reserves, a multiplier series with the base as its denominator is obviously a much smaller

---

procedures themselves (for example, the two-week lag in reserve accounting and the administrative procedures governing borrowing at the discount window). Short-run variations in the multiplier are certainly conditioned by the reserve-accounting and discount-window arrangements currently in force. It is not true, however, that variations in the multiplier due to nonpolicy disturbances would be negligible under, say, contemporaneous reserve accounting with a penalty discount rate tied to the federal funds rate. See chapter 6 for further discussion.

3. The target paths for the money stock are specified in seasonally adjusted terms. The transactions of the Federal Reserve in its open-market operations are, of course, not seasonally adjusted. The Federal Reserve must estimate and then try to offset seasonal factors when aiming for its seasonally adjusted target. If reserve-supplying or reserve-contracting operations are to be carried out to offset changes in reserve requirements, the Federal Reserve must explicitly decide about the size and timing of those actions; no mere mechanical calculation of the reserve effects of the changes in requirements is a sufficient guideline for actual transactions.

4. See James M. Johannes and Robert H. Rasche, "Predicting the Money Multiplier," *Journal of Monetary Economics,* vol. 5 (July 1979), pp. 301–25; Johannes and Rasche, "Can the Reserves Approach to Monetary Control Really Work?" *Journal of Money, Credit and Banking,* vol. 13 (August 1981), pp. 298–313; and Anatol B. Balbach, "How Controllable Is Money Growth?" *Federal Reserve Bank of St. Louis Review* (April 1981), pp. 3–12.

5. The multiplier series for M1 plotted by the Federal Reserve Bank of Saint Louis in its weekly release, *U.S. Financial Data,* is a prime example.

Figure 5-2. *Money Multiplier Linking M1 and Unborrowed Reserves, December 1976 through June 1982*[a]

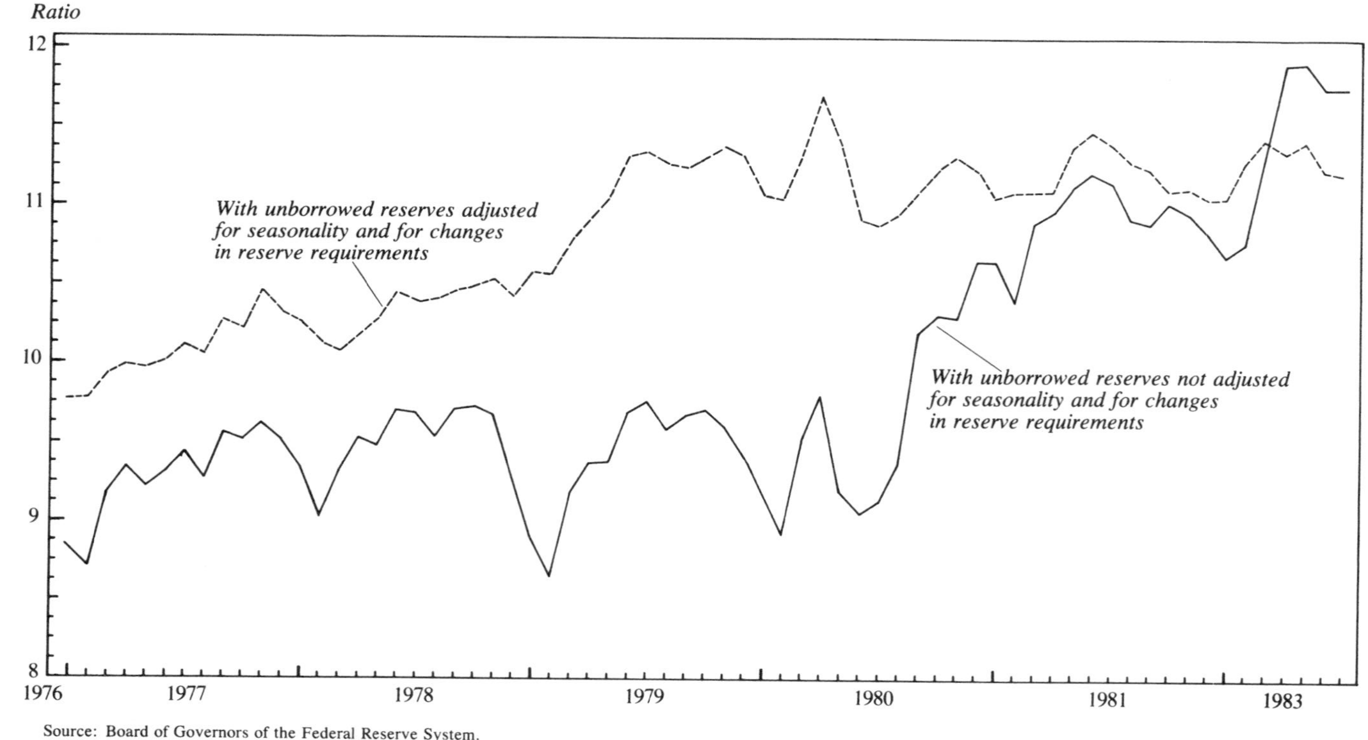

Source: Board of Governors of the Federal Reserve System.

a. The multiplier is defined as the ratio of M1 to unborrowed reserves (monthly averages of daily data).

number than a reserve multiplier. The base multiplier may superficially appear to be less variable, especially if plotted with a vertical scale that dampens the visual impression of variability.[6]

In terms of their effects on the money stock, however, the variations in the base multiplier are analytically significant. This fact is readily apparent in table 5-2 and figure 5-3, which repeat the earlier calculations but substitute the monetary base and the base multiplier for unborrowed reserves and the unborrowed reserves multiplier. The dominating influence on the base of the moderately regular growth of currency in circulation is responsible for the consistently positive and relatively smooth pattern of the numbers in column 3 of table 5-2 (shown as the dashed line in figure 5-3).[7] Note, however, that the qualitative conclusions emerging from table 5-2 and figure 5-3 are essentially the same as those evident in the earlier calculations using unborrowed reserves. In particular, changes in the money stock attributable to variations in the base multiplier are typically a major part of the actual change in money itself and often work to offset the effects on the money stock of changes in the base.

In addition to the evidence in table 5-2, there is an even more fundamental reason to doubt that a base multiplier would be an obviously more reliable fulcrum for controlling the money stock. The historical data for the base and the money stock were generated during periods when the Federal Reserve implemented policy with either the funds-rate regime or (since October 1979) the unborrowed-reserves regime.

Under either of those regimes most types of nonpolicy disturbance affect the money stock and the base in the same direction; see chapter 2 and appendix A. This positive correlation has tended to dampen variation

6. In June 1982 the outstanding amounts of unborrowed reserves (adjusted for changes in reserve requirements), discount-window borrowings, and currency in circulation were, respectively, $40.24 billion, $1.20 billion, and $128.40 billion. The adjusted monetary base—defined as the sum of adjusted unborrowed reserves, borrowing, currency in circulation, and vault cash at depository institutions not used to satisfy reserve requirements—was $172.1 billion. The M1 definition of the money stock was $451.3 billion. The multiplier for adjusted unborrowed reserves in figure 5-2 varied between roughly 9.5 and 11.7 during 1977–82. The multiplier for the adjusted monetary base over this period varied between roughly 2.60 and 2.73. (These calculations use the data adjusted for changes in reserve requirements by the Federal Reserve Board, available as of July 1982, rather than the similar data prepared by the Federal Reserve Bank of Saint Louis. For the points made in the text, however, it is immaterial whether one uses the data from the Board or the Federal Reserve Bank of Saint Louis.)

7. Figure 4-4 shows the currency component of the base.

Table 5-2. *Decomposition of Changes in M1 with the Monetary Base as High-Powered Money, September 1979 through June 1982*[a]
Billions of dollars

Year and month	*Change in money (sum of columns 2 and 3)* *(1)*	*Attributable to changes in the multiplier* *(2)*	*Attributable to changes in high-powered money* *(3)*
1979			
September	2.1	−1.1	3.2
October	1.2	−1.8	3.0
November	0.4	−1.5	1.9
December	2.1	−0.3	2.4
1980			
January	2.9	−0.6	3.5
February	3.2	1.1	2.1
March	0.0	−2.4	2.4
April	−5.2	−5.7	0.5
May	−0.9	−3.8	2.9
June	4.7	2.6	2.1
July	4.3	1.4	2.9
August	7.1	2.6	4.5
September	5.6	2.7	2.9
October	4.8	1.3	3.5
November	2.0	−3.6	5.6
December	−3.0	−4.3	1.3
1981			
January	3.4	2.9	0.5
February	1.5	−0.3	1.8
March	5.0	3.7	1.3
April	8.9	5.7	3.2
May	−4.1	−5.7	1.6
June	−0.8	−1.6	0.8
July	1.0	−1.1	2.1
August	1.7	0.6	1.1
September	0.1	−2.0	2.1
October	1.7	1.4	0.3
November	3.5	2.2	1.3
December	4.5	0.5	4.0
1982			
January	7.7	3.4	4.3
February	−1.3	−2.6	1.3
March	1.0	−0.6	1.6
April	4.0	0.5	3.5
May	−0.8	−4.0	3.2
June	−0.5	−3.4	2.9

Source: Same as table 5-1.

a. See table 5-1, note a. For the purposes of this table, high-powered money is defined as the monetary base (total reserves plus currency in circulation) adjusted by the staff of the Federal Reserve Board for changes in reserve requirements; the multiplier is the ratio of M1 to this adjusted monetary base.

Figure 5-3. *Decomposition of Changes in M1 with Adjusted Monetary Base as High-Powered Money, June 1979 through June 1982*

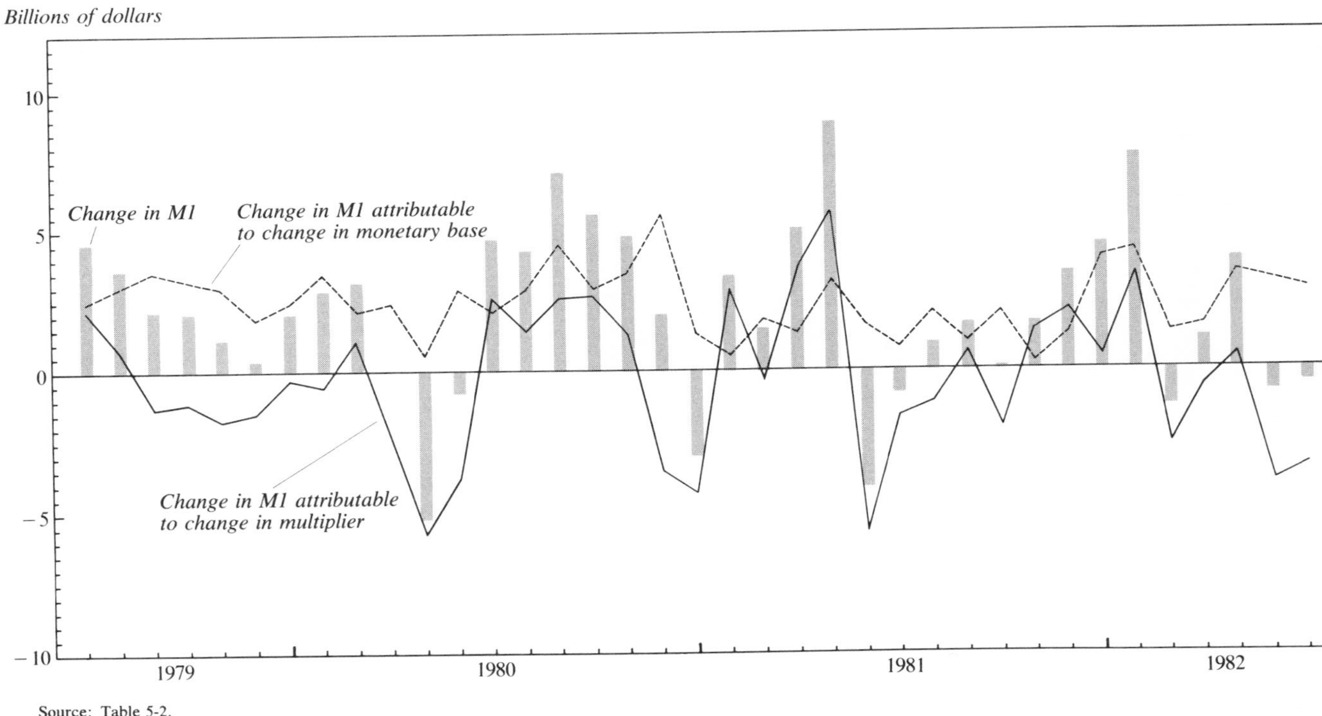

Source: Table 5-2.

in the historically observed data for the base multiplier. If the Federal Reserve decided to implement policy with the base regime, however, it would set the base along a predetermined path and nonpolicy disturbances would *not* generate movements in the base parallel to those in the money stock. The apparent greater predictability of the base multiplier could then prove to be ephemeral![8]

Simple though they are, the facts cited above expose the lack of a foundation for views de-emphasizing variations in the money multiplier. The awkward truth is that one needs considerably more information than changes in the balance sheet of the monetary authorities to be able to predict month-to-month or even quarter-to-quarter changes in the money stock.

8. The argument in this paragraph is developed in greater detail in David E. Lindsey, "Nonborrowed Reserve Targeting and Monetary Control," in Lawrence Meyer, ed., *Improving Money Stock Control: Problems, Solutions, and Consequences* (Federal Reserve Bank of St. Louis, 1982); and in Lindsey and others, "Monetary Control Experience Under the New Operating Procedures" in Board of Governors of the Federal Reserve System, *New Monetary Control Procedures*, vol. 2 (The Board, 1981).

CHAPTER SIX

Reform the Federal Reserve's Operating Procedures?

FUNDAMENTAL POINTS about the Federal Reserve's operating procedures and short-run control of the money stock are emphasized in chapters 2 through 5. Those chapters accordingly suppress many institutional details about the conduct of monetary policy. Some critics of the Federal Reserve, however, believe that part of this detail has major consequences for control of the money stock. This chapter thus reconsiders the conclusions reached earlier and asks, in particular, whether the prospects for close short-run control of the money stock could be radically transformed by modification of the Federal Reserve's operating procedures.

Reserve Accounting and Management of the Discount Window

In 1968 the Federal Reserve changed its regulations governing the maintenance of required reserves against deposits. Before the change (effective September 12, 1968), banks maintained required reserves on a "contemporaneous" basis; that is, an increase in average deposits during a current banking week resulted in an increase in required reserves *to be held during the current banking week.* After September 1968, however, banks were permitted to fulfill their reserve requirements on a "lagged" rather than contemporaneous basis; the banks based their calculations of required reserves held during a current banking week on the weekly average of reservable liabilities during the banking week *two weeks earlier.*[1]

1. The 1968 changes also provided that banks could satisfy reserve requirements in

The 1968 decision to introduce lagged reserve accounting was controversial, both within and outside the Federal Reserve System. Outside the Federal Reserve, the banks tended to favor lagged accounting; academic observers, especially those focusing on control of the money stock, tended to criticize it. The strongest critics of the 1968 decision asserted that short-run fluctuations in money could be very much smaller if the Federal Reserve would restore contemporaneous reserve accounting.[2]

a current maintenance period by vault cash held two weeks earlier and carry forward for one week a part or all of their reserve deficit or surplus in the current period (up to a maximum of 2 percent of required reserves).

2. The most detailed discussions of reserve-accounting procedures are contained in Federal Reserve documents. See, in particular, memorandum, S. M. Axilrod to Board of Governors of the Federal Reserve System, "Contemporaneous Reserve Requirements: A Review of Operational and Monetary Control Considerations," including memorandum from Peter A. Tinsley and others to the Board, "Estimated Monetary Policy Consequences of Reserve Accounting Procedures," September 14, 1981; memorandum, S. M. Axilrod, David Lindsey, and Myron Kwast to the Board, "Summary of Advantages and Disadvantages of CRR Alternatives," October 29, 1981; memorandum, S. M. Axilrod and others to the Board, "Evaluation of Comments on Staff Proposal for Contemporaneous Reserve Requirements and Staff Recommendations," June 23, 1982; and memorandum, Myron Kwast, Michelle Campbell, and Richard Field to the Board, "Summary of Comments on Board Staff Proposal for Contemporaneous Reserve Requirements," June 23, 1982. The preceding memoranda, prepared by the Federal Reserve Board staff, are obtainable through the Board's Freedom of Information office. The academic literature discussing the 1968 decision on reserve accounting is extensive; a selected list of references includes the University of Chicago Ph.D. dissertation of Warren L. Coats, Jr., partly summarized in "Lagged Reserve Accounting and the Money Supply Mechanism," *Journal of Money, Credit and Banking*, vol. 8 (May 1976), pp. 167–80; William Poole and Charles Lieberman, "Improving Monetary Control," *Brookings Papers on Economic Activity, 2:1972*, pp. 293–342; Daniel E. Laufenberg, "Contemporaneous versus Lagged Reserve Accounting," *Journal of Money, Credit and Banking*, vol. 8 (May 1976), pp. 239–45; Edgar L. Feige and Robert McGee, "Money Supply Control and Lagged Reserve Accounting," *Journal of Money, Credit and Banking*, vol. 9 (November 1977), pp. 536–51; Stephen F. LeRoy, "Monetary Control Under Lagged Reserve Accounting," *Southern Economic Journal*, vol. 46 (October 1979), pp. 460–70; Robert D. Laurent, "Reserve Requirements: Are They Lagged in the Wrong Direction?" *Journal of Money, Credit and Banking*, vol. 11 (August 1979), pp. 301–10; Warren L. Coats, Jr., "How To Improve Control of the Money Supply," *AEI Economist* (March 1981), pp. 1–12; David E. Lindsey, "Nonborrowed Reserve Targeting and Monetary Control," in Lawrence Meyer, ed., *Improving Money Stock Control: Problems, Solutions, and Consequences* (Federal Reserve Bank of St. Louis, 1982); Milton Friedman, "Monetary Policy: Theory and Practice," *Journal of Money, Credit and Banking*, vol. 14 (February 1982), pp. 98–118; William Poole, "Federal Reserve Operating Procedures: A Survey and Evaluation of the Historical Record Since October 1979," *Journal of Money, Credit and Banking*, vol. 14 (November 1982), pt. 2, pp. 575–96; and Vefa Tarhan and Paul A. Spindt, "Bank Earning Asset Behavior

Administrative management of the discount window is another aspect of Federal Reserve operating procedures that has frequently attracted outside criticism. The Federal Reserve itself takes the position that it would be undesirable for each member bank to be free to borrow without restriction:

> A pattern of large and volatile borrowing by the member banks would run the risk of eroding the System's ability to control bank reserves and thereby to influence growth of money and credit in line with the Nation's economic objectives. For these reasons administrative constraints on member bank borrowing have been developed. . . . most of the borrowing by member banks from the Reserve Banks is for quite short periods—usually no more than a few days—as banks seek funds to make temporary adjustments in their reserves. Such borrowing can be termed adjustment credit. Reasons for such borrowing that are considered appropriate generally include unexpected increases in loan demand, sudden deposit losses, or temporary and unexpected difficulties in obtaining funds through the facilities of the money market. Borrowing for the following purposes would be considered inappropriate: to finance speculative loans and investments, to substitute Federal Reserve credit for member bank capital, to finance lending in the Federal funds market, to acquire securities or other money market paper at a profit, or to refinance existing indebtedness to private lenders at the lower discount rate.
>
> In judging whether a member bank is relying unduly on borrowing at the discount window, the Reserve Bank discount officer takes into account the amount of a member's indebtedness in relation to its required reserves, the frequency of the bank's borrowing, any need for funds that is attributable to computer breakdowns in transfers of the funds, and any special circumstances affecting the current position of the bank.[3]

Many of those who criticize the management of the discount window in effect push the Federal Reserve's position even further. The critics assert that the banks, despite administrative constraints, can borrow (or repay) too freely and thereby partially offset Federal Reserve open-market operations that withdraw (or inject) reserves. For these critics, the discount window as presently administered introduces an undesirable degree of slippage into control of the money stock.

Like reserve accounting, the management of the discount window has generated considerable controversy over the years. The Federal Reserve itself has periodically reviewed the issues.[4] Outside critics have

---

and Causality Between Reserves and Money: Lagged versus Contemporaneous Accounting," *Journal of Monetary Economics* (forthcoming).

3. Board of Governors of the Federal Reserve System, *The Federal Reserve System: Purposes and Functions*, 6th ed. (The Board, 1974), p. 72.

4. For example, a Federal Reserve System committee issued a report and a series

favored one or another reform.[5] The most popular proposal with outside critics would require the Federal Reserve to "tie" the discount rate to the federal funds rate at a penalty surcharge (say, of 100 basis points or more). Banks would be allowed to borrow any amount, without administrative constraint, at the penalty discount rate. Some believe that this discount-window reform would also facilitate much closer short-run control of the money stock.

How should one assess these proposals for reform of reserve accounting procedures and administration of the discount window? One possible basis for evaluation—the one intended by many of their proponents—is to focus on the contribution of the reforms to money-stock control.

Judged in the light of that single criterion, the restoration of contemporaneous reserve accounting would probably be somewhat beneficial. At any rate, the studies focusing on the relative merits of lagged versus contemporaneous accounting have reached that conclusion. The most careful studies have been carried out by the Federal Reserve staff.[6] All the analyses point out that, subsequent to a nonpolicy disturbance pushing the money stock away from a target path, adjustment by banks of their reserve positions would take place somewhat more promptly under contemporaneous than under lagged accounting. That speedup in the banks' adjustment would in turn facilitate the Federal Reserve's short-run control of money.

Restoration of contemporaneous reserve accounting would impose additional costs on the depository institutions holding required reserves.

---

of studies in 1971; see Board of Governors of the Federal Reserve System, *Reappraisal of the Federal Reserve Discount Mechanism*, 3 vols. (August 1971); the paper by David Jones in volume 2 ("A Review of Recent Academic Literature on the Discount Mechanism") contains a lengthy bibliography. For a recent Federal Reserve staff review, see Peter Keir, "Impact of Discount Policy Procedures on the Effectiveness of Reserve Targeting," in Board of Governors of the Federal Reserve System, *New Monetary Control Procedures*, vol. 1 (The Board, 1981).

5. Recent commentary includes Perry D. Quick, "Federal Reserve Discount Window Procedures and Monetary Control: Two Modest Proposals," unpublished manuscript (1981); Warren L. Coats, Jr., "How to Improve Control of the Money Supply"; Milton Friedman, "Monetary Policy: Theory and Practice"; and Allan H. Meltzer, "Consequences of the Federal Reserve's Re-attachment to Free Reserves," paper presented at the 1981 annual meeting of the Western Economic Association (revised October 1981).

6. See especially Peter A. Tinsley and others, "Estimated Monetary Policy Consequences of Reserve Accounting Procedures," September 14, 1981; and David E. Lindsey and others, "Monetary Control Experience Under the New Operating Procedures," in *New Monetary Control Procedures*, Board of Governors, vol. 2.

In particular, the depository institutions would have to revise their existing computer and accounting procedures for collecting data on their deposits and for managing their reserve positions. Primarily because of these additional costs, most depository institutions have opposed a restoration of contemporaneous accounting.[7]

The additional costs to depository institutions associated with a return to contemporaneous reserve accounting would probably be largely transitory (while new procedures were being implemented). Viewed from a national perspective, moreover, the incremental costs seem modest. Contemporaneous reserve accounting seems likely to be benign in most other respects. All things considered, therefore, the marginal benefits to short-run control of the money stock constitute a reasonably persuasive case for moving back to contemporaneous reserve accounting (despite the fact, discussed below, that improving money-stock control is *not* the only criterion by which such reforms should be judged).

When the Federal Reserve Board acted in August 1980 to revise its regulations in accordance with the Monetary Control Act of 1980, it indicated that it was "disposed toward returning to contemporaneous reserve accounting . . . if further investigation indicates that such a system is operationally practical." On November 9, 1981, the Board requested public comments on a proposal to adopt a nearly contemporaneous accounting procedure.[8] At a meeting held in late June 1982, a majority of Board members indicated an intent to implement some variant of the November 1981 proposal. A second Board meeting in July resolved some but not all of the remaining technical details. In late September 1982 a Board meeting approved a final version of the proposal for implementation in February 1984.

The case for changing the procedures governing the discount rate and discount-window borrowing is more mixed. Tying the discount rate to the federal funds rate at a penalty surcharge would, it is true, severely

7. See Kwast, Campbell, and Field, "Summary of Comments on Board Staff Proposal for Contemporaneous Reserve Requirements."

8. The Board staff proposal recommended that required reserves be held during two-week maintenance periods, that those periods continue to end on Wednesday, that all depository institutions settle their reserve accounts at the same time, that required reserves be computed on the basis of average deposit levels over a two-week period ending on Monday, and that reserves required against transactions deposits be held in the maintenance period ending on the Wednesday *two days* after the end of the computation period. (The proposal recommended that required reserves against other reservable liabilities continue to be held on a lagged *two-week* rather than two-day basis.) See Federal Reserve System, press release, November 9, 1981.

restrict discount-window borrowing. But it is not invariably desirable to restrict such borrowing (see chapter 2 and the discussion below). Moreover, even if one focuses exclusively on the implications for money-stock control, a tied penalty rate might not prove beneficial. Careful analysis of the tied penalty rate by the Federal Reserve staff suggests that this reform would do little if anything to facilitate control of the money stock under a total-reserves regime whereas it would worsen control of money under the unborrowed-reserves regime. Under both those regimes a tied penalty rate would increase the short-run volatility of interest rates.[9]

A stronger case seems to exist for eliminating the administrative constraints and judgments applied at the window and substituting in their place a graduated structure of discount rates.[10] According to that proposal, prespecified quantitative limits would be established for the amount a bank could borrow at each of the lower steps of the graduated rate structure; at the top rate, which would be a penalty rate, there would be no limit (apart from the regular standards of prudent Reserve Bank lending on the basis of adequate collateral). Such a graduated structure of discount rates might encounter legal difficulties.[11] If it could be implemented, however, this rate structure would improve the accuracy of Federal Reserve forecasts of borrowing (which in turn would facilitate money-stock control) yet permit borrowing to continue to play a role as a short-run "shock absorber" for nonpolicy disturbances in the financial markets.

It is not feasible to present a more detailed review here of alternative reforms for reserve accounting and administration of the discount window. Instead, what needs to be stressed is that such reforms are not of overriding consequence for the conduct of monetary policy. Nor are they a sufficient condition for achieving close short-run control of the money stock. I know of no theoretical analysis nor any empirical

9. See Tinsley and others, "Estimated Monetary Policy Consequences of Reserve-Accounting Procedures" and Tinsley and others, "Policy Robustness: Specification and Simulation of a Monthly Money Market Model," *Journal of Money, Credit and Banking*, vol. 14 (November 1982), pt. 2, pp. 829–56. On these points, see also Keir, "Impact of Discount Policy Procedures on the Effectiveness of Reserve Targeting." The tied penalty rate, if implemented at all, should only be implemented in conjunction with contemporaneous reserve accounting; see Quick, "Federal Reserve Discount Window Procedures."

10. See, for example, Quick, "Federal Reserve Discount Window Procedures."

11. See the discussion in Keir, "Impact of Discount Policy Procedures on the Effectiveness of Reserve Targeting."

evidence convincingly demonstrating that such reforms can give the Federal Reserve *much* greater precision in controlling the money stock. The reforms can be incrementally—but only incrementally—helpful. Enthusiastic protagonists of the reforms often claim a great deal too much for them.[12] The essential point is that nonpolicy disturbances would still inevitably push the money stock up or down in the short run, and could still easily produce an "erratic" short-run pattern of money growth.

When proposing modifications in reserve-accounting and discount-window arrangements, critics of the Federal Reserve should also remember that reforms could have some counterproductive as well as beneficial effects on money-stock control. In particular, if discount-window credit were available to banks on only penalty terms, banks could significantly alter their behavior in holding excess reserves. If the banks were to hold larger excess reserves on average and were to vary their holdings to a greater extent than at present, that behavior would, other things being equal, worsen short-run control of the money stock.

Shift to a Total-Reserves Regime or a Base Regime?

What about an even more fundamental reform in Federal Reserve procedures, a change in the operating regime itself? In particular, suppose the Federal Reserve were to use total reserves or the monetary base as its main policy instrument rather than, as at present (since October 1979), unborrowed reserves.

The view that the total-reserves or the base regime would be unambiguously preferable to the unborrowed-reserves regime is often espoused by monetarist critics of the Federal Reserve. For example, Allan Meltzer, James Johannes, and Robert Rasche have strongly advocated use of the base regime.[13]

As already suggested by the analysis in chapter 3, one basic difficulty with this position is that it tends to compare operating regimes without giving adequate attention to all types of nonpolicy disturbances.

12. More careful advocates do not make this mistake. See, for example, Poole, "Federal Reserve Operating Procedures."

13. See Meltzer, "Consequences of the Federal Reserve's Re-attachment to Free Reserves"; James M. Johannes and Robert H. Rasche, "Can the Reserves Approach to Monetary Control Really Work?" *Journal of Money, Credit and Banking*, vol. 13 (August 1981), pp. 298–313.

Recall first that if it were reasonable to ignore all types of nonpolicy disturbances other than unexpected, real-sector events causing aggregate demand to rise or fall, the case for the superiority of the base regime over the unborrowed-reserves regime would be beyond reproach. (Such relevant events would include not only nonpolicy surprises in goods and labor markets but also mistakes or irresponsible decisions in the execution of fiscal policy.) For the reasons summarized in chapter 2, in the presence of disturbances originating in the real sectors of the economy the base regime permits larger changes in interest rates and does more to inhibit the procyclical movements of the money stock than the unborrowed-reserves regime. Because of this greater frictional resistance to the fluctuations in aggregate demand, the base regime more effectively mitigates the adverse consequences of the underlying disturbances originating in the real sectors.

The movements of borrowing at the Federal Reserve discount window tend to be singled out for critical attention in this analysis of unexpected real-sector events. When the Federal Reserve leaves the discount rate unchanged as the funds rate begins to rise in response to a surge in aggregate demand, for example, banks borrow more at the discount window. Other things being equal, this increase in borrowing helps to restrain the size of the rise in the interest rate, which in turn permits a larger procyclical increase in the money stock than would otherwise occur. Under these circumstances, it has been correctly pointed out, the buffering or escape-valve aspect of discount-window borrowing is *not* constructive.[14]

The problem with typical monetarist analyses along these lines is their tendency to focus only on real-sector disturbances causing changes in aggregate demand. To be complete, analysis must go further and consider other types of disturbance. As soon as other types are considered,

14. As can be seen from a comparison of equations A-12 and A-14 and table A-6 in appendix A, the analysis of this type of disturbance under the base and the unborrowed-reserves regimes is more complex than is commonly recognized. In particular, borrowing at the discount window is not in any clear sense the villain causing the unborrowed-reserves regime to produce poorer results. When the funds rate rises more under the base regime than under the unborrowed-reserves regime, borrowing also rises *more* under the base regime. The base regime is associated with a larger rise in the funds rate because the base itself is not permitted to increase (despite the increase in borrowing); induced open-market sales of securities are required to keep the base unchanged. Under the unborrowed-reserves regime, on the other hand, the increase in borrowing can increase the base, which in turn helps to dampen the extent of the rise in the funds rate.

however, the "unambiguous" superiority of the base regime becomes ambiguous (see chapter 3).

Unqualified criticism of the Federal Reserve's policy for discount-window borrowing likewise becomes difficult to sustain. Recall again from chapter 2 the cases of unexpected changes in the banks' demand for excess reserves and unexpected shifts in the asset preferences of nonbanks for deposits. For those types of disturbance, the role of discount-window borrowing as an escape valve is highly constructive. Changes in borrowing are a *preferred* destination of the underlying shocks: they serve as shock absorbers.[15]

The base and the total-reserves regimes have the characteristic that they automatically induce open-market operations that tend to offset changes in borrowing. The unborrowed-reserves and portfolio regimes do not have this characteristic. But how can it be correct to infer that the regimes tending to offset borrowing are on that account clearly superior? The uncomfortable fact is that the shock-absorber role of borrowing is sometimes appropriate and at other times is not.

To argue convincingly that the base regime dominates the unborrowed-reserves regime would require, at the very least, some evidence that disturbances in banks' reserves demands and in nonbanks' asset preferences for deposits and currency are typically smaller, more transitory, and less frequent than other types of disturbance. Such evidence could come to light in the future. It does not exist now. As shown in chapters 4 and 5, moreover, evidence does exist to contradict the presumption that disturbances originating in the money market are small enough to be ignored.

The second basic difficulty with the monetarist case for a shift in operating procedures to a total-reserves or a base regime is the tendency to evaluate regimes only in terms of their contribution to controlling the money stock. A preoccupation with improving short-run control of money is a similar shortcoming of monetarist analyses of reserve-accounting and discount-window arrangements.

Control of the money stock is, at best, only a surrogate objective for the Federal Reserve. That surrogate objective, furthermore, is not invariably compatible with the fundamental objectives of Federal Re-

15. In contrast, when an unexpected change occurs in banks' willingness to borrow at the discount window, such a shock will have unfavorable consequences if transmitted to interest rates and the money stock (see table 2-3). The unborrowed-reserves regime permits such a transmission. The base regime does not.

serve policy (see chapter 8). It is inappropriate, therefore, to judge reforms in operating procedures solely in terms of their potential contribution to controlling money.

Keeping the Federal Reserve's Operating Procedures in Perspective

One of my main purposes throughout chapters 2 through 6 has been to emphasize that the United States has a financial system that does not lend itself—and even with reforms in Federal Reserve operating procedures would not lend itself—to precise short-run control of the money stock.

I have focused the discussion on the nonpolicy determinants of money because those determinants are so often ignored or underemphasized. There is some risk, however, that this effort to correct misimpressions may itself be misunderstood. To conclude this part of the argument, therefore, I want to acknowledge again the extremely important role played by the Federal Reserve in determining the money stock, even in the short run. It is a disservice either to emphasize the nonpolicy determinants of the money stock to the exclusion of the influence of Federal Reserve actions or to pretend that the nonpolicy factors can be easily overcome in the short run by offsetting Federal Reserve actions.

The unexciting truth is that the question of how much short-run control the Federal Reserve can exert over the money stock has no business being on the agenda of controversial issues about the conduct of monetary policy.

CHAPTER SEVEN

Control of the Money Stock over the Medium and Long Run

CLOSE CONTROL of money, defined as continuous prevention of sizable deviations of money from a predetermined target path, is shown in chapters 4 through 6 to be impossible over a short-run period of two to three months. This chapter briefly discusses whether the Federal Reserve can closely control the money stock over longer horizons and, if so, in what sense of "closely."

Averaging Control over the Medium and Long Run

Suppose first that the temporal reference period for evaluating control is extended to an interval as long as, say, four to six months. I will call this period the medium run.

Over such a period there is a sense in which it becomes possible for the Federal Reserve to achieve moderately close control of (at least some definitions of) the money stock. This sense, however, is quite different from *continuous* prevention of sizable deviations of money from a target path. Rather, the possibility involves bringing the *average* value of the money stock measured over the four to six months close to the *average* value of the target path for the same period.

To achieve "averaging control," the Federal Reserve must continuously monitor the inevitable short-run deviations of the actual money stock from target path and make frequent, short-run adjustments in the settings for its policy instruments to try to move money toward its average target value. (As time passes during the medium-run reference period, the average value of the target path itself changes—at a smooth exponential rate if the target path has been derived from a simple growth rate.)

Averaging the value of the money stock over an extended period washes out shorter-run fluctuations. Comparing the discrepancy between such an average and the period average of the target path nets temporary overshoots and temporary shortfalls; for example, if the actual money stock remains well above the target path for several months and then falls well below the target path for several months, the averages of the actual stock and the target path may nonetheless be nearly identical for the medium-run period as a whole. The longer the medium-run period over which the averages are taken, the larger the weight implicitly assigned in the calculation to the mean difference between the actual and the target paths and the smaller the weight assigned to the variance of the actual path around the target path.

If the ability of the Federal Reserve to control the money stock is appraised exclusively in terms of the mean difference between the actual and the target paths, the extent of potential control can be said to be greater the longer the reference period. This averaging concept of the controllability of money, however, is deceptive. It invites the essentially superficial observation that the Federal Reserve can control the money stock very closely over a long-run period. This observation is superficial because it begs entirely the question of whether, and if so how much, the variability of the money stock during the reference period matters. If an averaging concept for controllability is the only standard for judgment and if the reference period can be arbitrarily chosen to be very long, the Federal Reserve can control virtually any single economic variable closely—including inflation, or employment, or the real value of national output!

In particular, suppose the time horizon for "averaging controllability" is extended to the long run, defined as a period of twelve months or more. Over that extended period the Federal Reserve undoubtedly can, if it gives priority to the objective, cause the value of the money stock averaged over the entire period to come quite close to the average value of a target path specified at the beginning of the period. "Quite close" in this context could mean, for example, a discrepancy between the actual and target averages of not more than 1.5 percent, and probably significantly less than that.[1]

1. Alternatively stated, for target growth *rates* in the range of, say, 3 to 10 percent a year, the achieved growth rate for the annual averages of money could fall within a range of plus or minus 1.5 percentage points around the target rate. For relevant calculations see, for example, David E. Lindsey and others, "Monetary Control

As stated above, this choice of a long reference period, and hence of a relatively emasculated definition of close control, merits much more critical scrutiny than it typically receives. But if this is the sort of thing that people want the Federal Reserve to do, the deed *can* be done.

Note that when the averaging definition of controllability and a reference period as long as twelve months are accepted as the relevant criteria for evaluation, the issues discussed in the preceding chapter become even less important. In particular, whether reserve accounting is lagged or contemporaneous and whether discount-window arrangements remain unchanged or are modified have only a small bearing on the ability of the Federal Reserve to achieve an annual average target for the money stock. It is *possible* to do the deed without reforms in operating procedures.

Control of the Money Stock and Variability in Interest Rates

Suppose the Federal Reserve adopted a policy of averaging control, defined over a sequence of reference periods of twelve months—say, successive calendar years—and suppose it paid exclusive attention to emerging discrepancies between the averages of the actual money stock and its target path over the portion of the calendar year already elapsed. Policy actions by the Federal Reserve would then continuously try to move money toward its average target value. Those policy actions would be designed to attain the average target value as promptly as possible (since by hypothesis the money stock would be the exclusive focus of policy). And those actions would aim at a temporary shortfall (overshoot) of money below the average target value to compensate for any net overshooting (undershooting) occurring earlier in the year.

This relatively mechanical control procedure would have several major consequences. It would require the Federal Reserve to ignore new information about other variables in the economy when choosing the settings for its policy instruments (see chapter 8). And it would require the Federal Reserve to ignore the trade-off that exists between the variability of the money stock about a target path and the variability of short-term interest rates.

Experience under the New Operating Procedures,'' in Board of Governors of the Federal Reserve System, *New Monetary Control Procedures*, vol. 2 (The Board, 1981).

This latter trade-off is carefully identified and empirically estimated in an important paper by Peter Tinsley and others.[2] As these authors show, the Federal Reserve has substantial discretion over how promptly it may try to get the money stock back to a target path. The faster it tries to move money back to target (the higher the "speed of reentry"), the greater its success in reducing deviations of money about the target path—*but at the expense of increasing the volatility of short-term interest rates*. This trade-off is estimated to exist even for the medium run, and is pronounced for a short-run period of two months or less.

2. Peter Tinsley and others, "Money Market Impacts of Alternative Operating Procedures," in *New Monetary Control Procedures*, vol. 2.

CHAPTER EIGHT

Should Policy Be Conducted with the Money Stock as an Intermediate Target?

MONETARISM as commonly understood emphasizes policy control of the money stock. Close control of money from month to month is not possible; close control over the medium or long run, in the sense of averaging control, is possible. The position adopted by pragmatic monetarists, therefore, insists at a minimum on successful realization of averaging control over a medium or long run. Most monetarists also urge the Federal Reserve to try in the short run to achieve a moving average level of the money stock that tracks a predetermined target path as closely as possible.

The contention that it is *desirable* to try to make the average value of money follow a target path over a medium-run or long-run horizon raises issues of substantially greater importance than any of those considered in previous chapters. In this chapter, I include a brief summary of these issues and my conclusions about them. My recent book provides a careful and detailed analysis.[1]

Advocacy of the strategy of using the money stock as an intermediate-target variable typically rests on two assertions:[2]

1. See Ralph C. Bryant, *Money and Monetary Policy in Interdependent Nations* (Brookings Institution, 1980), especially part 4. The original work criticizing intermediate-target strategies includes John H. Kareken, Thomas Muench, and Neil Wallace, "Optimal Open Market Strategy: The Use of Information Variables," *American Economic Review*, vol. 63 (March 1973), pp. 156–72; Roger N. Waud, "Proximate Targets and Monetary Policy," *Economic Journal*, vol. 83 (March 1973), pp. 1–20; Benjamin M. Friedman, "Targets, Instruments, and Indicators of Monetary Policy," *Journal of Monetary Economics*, vol. 1 (October 1975), pp. 443–73; and Stephen F. LeRoy and Roger N. Waud, "Observability, Measurement Error, and the Optimal Use of Information for Monetary Policy," Special Studies Paper 72 (Federal Reserve Board, Division of Research and Statistics, October 1975).

2. Bryant, *Money and Monetary Policy in Interdependent Nations*, p. 69. See also the discussion on pp. 69–71.

There exists for the economy as a whole a particular bundle of financial assets—the money stock—reliably linked through one or more behavioral relationships to the ultimate-target variables of national economic policy; knowledge about these relationships is markedly less uncertain than knowledge about the other macroeconomic behavioral relationships constituting the structure of the economy [the reliability proposition].

Policymakers are able to adjust the actual instruments of monetary policy so as closely to control the money stock [the controllability proposition].

From these propositions it is clear that at least two criteria are relevant to the choice of a "best" definition of money to use as an intermediate target. The reliability proposition argues for selecting that definition for which the causal linkages between money and ultimate target variables are least uncertain. The controllability proposition suggests choosing the financial aggregate that can be most easily controlled.

One difficulty is immediately evident: the two criteria point in opposite directions. If the Federal Reserve searches for the financial aggregate most reliably linked by behavioral relations (for example, the demand-for-money function) to ultimate target variables, it tends, figuratively speaking, to move further and further in the direction of ultimate targets along the chains of causal relations in the behavioral functions characterizing the economy. The more reliable is an aggregate in its links to ultimate targets, the less closely it can be controlled by adjustment of the instruments of monetary policy. Conversely, the more closely an aggregate is tied to policy instruments, the more complex and numerous the behavioral relations between it and the ultimate target variables. Thus the price paid for selecting an aggregate that can be controlled closely is to accept increased uncertainty about the linkages between that aggregate and the ultimate targets.

The Federal Reserve does not have a straightforward basis for trading off controllability and reliability when selecting an intermediate-target variable. There is thus no straightforward basis for choosing the "best" definition of money for use as a policy target.

In my view this dilemma does not warrant extensive research to clarify criteria for choosing the best definition of the money stock for use as an intermediate target. In the absence of the intermediate-target motive for identifying a best definition of money, the definition of monetary aggregates becomes an issue of secondary importance for monetary policy. Furthermore, one easily loses sight of the issues of genuine importance to policy in the miasma of technical details about the differences among alternative definitions of money.

To focus on the genuine issues, one should set aside the definitional dilemma and consider the intrinsic merits of an intermediate-target strategy on the assumption that the definition of money has already been selected in the most appropriate way possible.

The complete decision problem facing the Federal Reserve is to select time sequences of settings for the actual instruments of policy that are judged most likely to bring about best feasible paths for ultimate-target variables. Intermediate-target strategies decompose the larger problem into two subordinate problems, with decisions at the two levels made separately and sequentially. The upper-level decision involves reasoning in a reverse direction from desired time paths for the ultimate targets back to a target path for the money stock. The lower-level decision takes that target path for money as given and determines time paths for the instrument settings designed to keep the actual money stock tracking as closely as possible along its target path.

Different periodicities of decisionmaking are presupposed for the two levels. Calculations of the target path for money at the upper level are revised only periodically (in an extreme variant, never); but lower-level decisions are revised more or less continuously in response to observed discrepancies between the actual money stock and its target path. A given upper-level specification of the target path for the money stock thus becomes a surrogate for the ultimate objectives and is the day-by-day operating objective of lower-level policy actions.

The dichotomization of policy decisions into two stages and the different periodicities of decisionmaking for the two stages are the key characteristics that differentiate an intermediate-target approach from alternative strategies for conducting policy.

Why might it be desirable to decompose the overall decision problem into two stages? What justifies the differences between the upper-level and lower-level periodicities of decisionmaking? An obvious alternative is to derive preferred time paths for policy instruments from the best feasible paths of the ultimate-target variables in a single-stage, integrated decision (for short, discretionary instrument adaptation) rather than interposing a two-stage process that pivots on an intermediate surrogate target.

Few advocates of an intermediate-target strategy pivoting on the money stock have provided a rationale for its two-stage characteristics. But six types of justification are conceivable. They assert that a money strategy (1) uses the flow of new information about the economy more efficiently, (2) copes more successfully with policymakers' uncertainty about how the economy functions, (3) incurs smaller resource costs, (4) provides better insulation for monetary policy from the vagaries of the political process, (5) affords better protection for the economy from errors due to incompetence or mistakes in judgment on the part of central bankers, and (6) takes better advantage of game-theoretic, expectational interactions between policymakers and the private sector.

It has been shown that each of those justifications is analytically inadequate. None of the last four is a convincing rationale for a two-stage decision process. And the first two are flatly wrong: a money strategy is demonstrably *less* efficient in processing new data about the economy and *less* successful in coping with uncertainty than a single-stage strategy of discretionary instrument adaptation.

The putative case for using the money stock as a surrogate target on information grounds appeals to the fact that data for the surrogate become available frequently and relatively promptly whereas ultimate-target variables are glimpsed only intermittently (GNP being observed, for example, only quarterly and with a substantial lag). Because of the better flow of data about the money stock, it is possible for the Federal Reserve to monitor closely the behavior of money relative to its target path and to try to correct promptly any incipient deviations. It is not possible to make continuous adjustments in policy in response to observed deviations of ultimate-target variables from their desired paths.

Only in a superficial and incorrect analysis, however, can those facts be cited as an argument in favor of a two-stage money strategy. The Federal Reserve should not use an intermediate variable as a surrogate target rather than aim at the genuine objectives merely because the former is continuously visible while the latter are not. The problem is analogous to that facing a ship's captain who must navigate into a harbor at night. It would not be logical to steer into a channel marked by buoys flashing every ten seconds rather than one marked by buoys flashing every two minutes merely because the former can be followed more easily. Useful information is obtained from a frequently flashing buoy because the captain can thereby establish his current location more exactly. But he should steer the ship into the channel marked by the ten-second buoys only if he believes that to be the correct route to his destination berth in the harbor.

The essence of the two-stage decision procedure is *not* to recalculate the upper-level target path for the money stock with each arrival of new information. Temporarily (or in an extreme variant, permanently), an intermediate-target strategy thus discards a large fraction of the available new data about the economy. And it does not react more promptly or more efficiently to any of the nondiscarded data than does a strategy of discretionary instrument adaptation. A careful analysis of how information is used in alternative strategies, far from supporting a money strategy, exposes serious inefficiencies inherent in the two-stage decision procedure.

When the flow of new data about the economy is inadequate and unreliable and when existing knowledge about behavioral relations is very imperfect (the analytical framework used by policymakers thus poorly imitating the true behavior of the economy), all strategies for conducting monetary policy will be problematic. The more deficient the information flow, the smaller may be the degree of superiority of a single-stage over an intermediate-target strategy. No conceivable flow of new information, however, could reverse the relative ranking of the two strategies from the perspective of efficiency in information processing.

A similar fallacy vitiates the argument that a money strategy copes more successfully with uncertainty. The existence of great uncertainty about how the economy functions, and in particular how it reacts to Federal Reserve policy actions, is a compelling reason for making policy decisions cautiously. But uncertainty scarcely constitutes a valid analytical reason for splitting the policy problem into two stages with different periodicities for the two levels of decisions. A two-stage approach necessarily ignores interdependencies between the uncertainties associated with upper-level and lower-level decisions. For equivalent assumptions about the forms and intensities of uncertainties confronting the Federal Reserve, about the Federal Reserve's ultimate objectives, and about its competence in making decisions, the results from pursuing a money strategy can never be better, and in the general case are unambiguously worse, than the results from following a strategy of discretionary instrument adaptation.[3]

Considerations of resource costs, although an important factor in the choice of an analytical framework for modeling the economy, do not have decisive implications for strategy choice. The putative justification

3. For detailed discussion of the inefficiencies in using new data and coping with uncertainty that are inherent in a two-stage decision process, see Bryant, *Money and Monetary Policy in Interdependent Nations*, chap. 17.

for a money strategy based on resource costs is not a convincing reason for using a surrogate money target in a two-stage decision process.[4]

The putative rationales for a money strategy that advocate insulation of monetary policy from the vagaries of the political process and from human error and the rationale that appeals to game-theoretic, expectational interactions with the private sector are essentially arguments against the exercise of discretion by the Federal Reserve. The "insulation" rationales bring in complex political and sociological issues, including the pros and cons of political independence for the Federal Reserve. The game-theoretic rationale, increasingly used in the context of the research on rational expectations, asserts that limits on the Federal Reserve's discretion, implemented by credible announcements of a policy rule, will induce agents in the private sector to make better decisions and hence lead to a more favorable evolution of the national economy.

The critical point in this context is that these arguments are conceivable justifications for a monetary-policy rule but are not persuasive justifications for a rule with respect to an intermediate-target variable.

Suppose the political grounds for espousing monetary-policy rules were accepted. Even then, such grounds would not justify a two-stage strategy focused on a *money* rule. Under a money strategy, even if the money target path is rigidly specified by a nondiscretionary rule, the Federal Reserve must exert continuous discretion to refix its instrument settings to try to keep the money stock on its target path. Thus political pressure might still be applied in an effort to coerce the Federal Reserve to aim its discretionary actions at political goals; the Federal Reserve could subtly yield to such pressures while still professing to be "trying" to adhere to the money rule. A money strategy also provides leeway for the Federal Reserve to make mistakes because of incompetence. With an instrument rule, on the other hand, an unambiguous check would exist on whether the rules were being followed; actual instrument settings would merely have to be compared with the settings dictated by the rule. Thus insulation either from politics or from human frailty would be better assured. Instrument rules, in short, would restrain discretionary policy mistakes altogether whereas a money-stock rule leaves the door partly open to discretionary errors. If discretion is thought undesirable, why not shut the door completely?

4. Ibid., chap. 16.

Similarly, if game-theoretic and expectational considerations are thought to justify the imposition of limits on Federal Reserve discretionary actions by announcement of a rule for monetary policy, why should the announcement be made in terms of an intermediate-target variable, the stock of money? One benefit of preannounced limits on discretionary action, if they were credible, would be a reduction of uncertainty in the private sector about future policy actions. But the greatest reduction in that uncertainty could be achieved by announcements of limits applying to the actual instruments of policy, to the ultimate objectives of the Federal Reserve, or conceivably to both. The instruments are controlled precisely; when an instrument setting is observed to change, the private sector knows the change has occurred because the Federal Reserve has made an explicit decision. Instrument decisions will be expected to change in the future only because of explicit policy decisions. Credible announcements of planned instrument settings would thus give private decisionmakers a firmer basis for formulating expectations and decisions.

No matter how vigorously the Federal Reserve pursues a money strategy, on the other hand, some deviations are inevitable between the actual money stock and a preannounced target path. When deviations are observed, moreover, economic units in the private sector cannot discern how much of the deviations should be attributed to nonpolicy factors outside the control of the Federal Reserve and how much to the Federal Reserve's failure in adhering conscientiously to the preannounced target path. The private sector should therefore value an announcement of an intermediate-target path less highly than correspondingly truthful announcements of instrument plans and ultimate objectives. An analogous point applies to the credibility of Federal Reserve announcements. If the Federal Reserve announces limits on its discretion in terms of instrument paths, decisionmakers in the private sector need only decide whether to believe that the Federal Reserve will adhere to the announced limits. If the announcement is of an intermediate-target path for the money stock, however, there is yet a further element of doubt about whether the money target path can be and therefore will be achieved.[5]

5. In principle the disadvantages of a money rule mentioned above could be offset by some countervailing advantages. For example, it could be argued that many economic units in the private sector can understand what "money" is and why it plays an important role in the economy and will therefore react favorably to a Federal Reserve

In summary, proponents of rules for the money stock who appeal to the insulation and game-theoretic justifications overlook a logical gap in their reasoning when they leap from general arguments against discretion to the specific recommendation of pegging the money stock on an intermediate-target path.[6]

To complete this overview of the objections to an intermediate-target strategy, three additional considerations deserve mention. First, the two-stage decision process of an intermediate-target strategy requires a policymaking model that can validly be decomposed into two submodels. In effect, the Federal Reserve must be able to segregate the causal links between its policy instruments and money from the causal links between money and ultimate-target variables and operate on the former independently of the latter. Economic theory raises substantial doubts, however, that macroeconomic behavior is sufficiently recursive to warrant the Federal Reserve using a model that assumes the required decomposability. This problem is a fundamental analytical weakness that has been overlooked by advocates of intermediate-target strategies.[7]

Second, the use of a surrogate money target can easily divert attention from ultimate economic objectives, with undesirable consequences for policy decisions. Economic units in the private sector may more readily misperceive monetary policy; as a result, desirable adjustments in policy may at times be more difficult. At worst, policymakers in the Federal Reserve themselves may slip into the habit of treating the money target path as an end in its own right.

Third, an intermediate-target strategy for monetary policy makes coordination of monetary policy and fiscal policy more difficult than it would otherwise be with monetary policy conducted by discretionary instrument adaptation. This consideration becomes progressively more important the stronger is the desire to use monetary and fiscal instruments in a unified discretionary approach to macroeconomic stabilization policy as a whole.

---

announcement of a money rule whereas they are not familiar with instrument variables such as bank reserves or the federal funds rate and will not react as favorably to announcements of an instrument rule. Such advantages of a money rule, it could be argued, might even be great enough to offset completely the disadvantages identified above. While this variant of the game-theoretic justification for a money rule could conceivably be valid, it seems strained and unpersuasive to me.

6. For further discussion, see Bryant, *Money and Monetary Policy in Interdependent Nations,* chap. 18.

7. Ibid., chaps. 6 and 16.

CHAPTER NINE

Federal Reserve Policy under the Constraint of Money Targets

TO RELATE previous chapters of this book to the actual conduct of Federal Reserve policy in recent years, I now turn to several further questions. To what extent—how rigidly or flexibly—has the Federal Reserve been following a two-stage money strategy? How significant was the October 1979 change in operating procedures? What is the least unsatisfactory way for the Federal Reserve to implement a money strategy if a political commitment to that approach is temporarily irreversible? Has the Federal Reserve performed well in setting and achieving money targets?

The Federal Reserve's Use of Money Targeting

The documents and statements released to the public by the Federal Reserve in recent years emphasize the behavior, past and prospective, of the money stock. In particular, the Federal Open Market Committee (FOMC) establishes target cones for money, applicable to calendar years, and gives prominence to the targets in the policy records of its meetings. At each regularly scheduled meeting, the FOMC has also set interim target paths applicable to the following two or three months.

When the Federal Reserve changed its operating procedures in October 1979, in effect switching from a funds-rate regime to an unborrowed-reserves regime, it restated its commitment to the use of money targets. To an extent not fully apparent at the time or now, the October 1979 change in operating regimes also represented a strengthening of the commitment to a money strategy.

It has been especially difficult for those outside the Federal Reserve to judge the details of its policy since the 1979 change in procedures. The policy record of each FOMC meeting became much less informative about the intended settings for the actual instruments of policy. The policy record continued to give quantitative descriptions of the annual and interim paths for the intermediate target(s)—that is, the various definitions of money.[1] But the reserve paths designed to achieve the money target paths were not identified. Nor did the policy record indicate, in its review of past developments, when or how the reserve paths had been adjusted between FOMC meetings.

To be sure, during 1981 and 1982 several documents became available that supplemented the information released in earlier policy records.[2] Nonetheless, in some important respects the details and nuances of policy remain vague. For example, outsiders cannot judge how much weight the FOMC gives to variables other than the monetary aggregates when instructing its manager for operations at meetings, or how much weight is given to variables other than money by the chairman of the FOMC and that manager when contemplating intermeeting adjustments in the path for unborrowed reserves.

Notwithstanding the uncertainty about details, it is clear that the Federal Reserve has been following a money strategy. It is also evident that the Federal Reserve has left itself considerable room for maneuver within the overall outlines of the strategy. In brief, there is a serious

1. Target paths have been specified for M1 (during 1980 and 1981, both M1A and M1B), M2, and M3. A target path has also been identified for a measure of bank credit.

2. The first detailed explanation of the October 1979 changes in procedures was given in a staff document, "The New Federal Reserve Technical Procedures for Controlling Money," January 30, 1980; this document also appeared as "Appendix B: Description of the New Procedures for Controlling Money," appended to the "Monetary Policy Report to Congress Pursuant to the Full Employment and Balanced Growth Act of 1978," February 19, 1980. The titles given to the document lend credence to the view that the October 1979 measures were intended as a strengthening of the commitment to money targets, not merely as a switch in operating regime. Subsequent documents on this subject include Stephen H. Axilrod and David E. Lindsey, "Federal Reserve System Implementation of Monetary Policy: Analytical Foundations of the New Approach," *American Economic Review*, vol. 71 (May 1981, *Papers and Proceedings, 1980*), pp. 246–52; Peter D. Sternlight and others, "Monetary Policy and Open Market Operations in 1980," *Federal Reserve Bank of New York Quarterly Review*, vol. 6 (Summer 1981), pp. 56–75; Board of Governors of the Federal Reserve System, *New Monetary Control Procedures*, 2 vols. (The Board, 1981)—(see especially the papers by Fred Levin and Paul Meek, David E. Lindsey and others, and Peter Keir); Peter D. Sternlight, "Monetary Policy and Open Market Operations in 1981," *Federal Reserve Bank of New York Quarterly Review*, vol. 7 (Spring 1982), pp. 34–53; and Stephen H. Axilrod, "Monetary Policy, Money Supply, and the Federal Reserve's Operating Procedures," *Federal Reserve Bulletin*, vol. 68 (January 1982), pp. 13–24.

commitment to the money stock as an intermediate target but that commitment is not rigid.

There are at least five elements of flexibility in the Federal Reserve's use of the two-stage approach. First, the target growth rate for a monetary aggregate is specified as a range rather than a single-valued path. Toward the end of a calendar year, the distance between the lower and upper boundaries of the resulting cone is considerable (see, for example, figure 4-1).

Second, when the Federal Reserve specifies a new target cone in the winter for the following calendar year, it tends to establish the base of the new cone as the recent average value of the *actual* money stock, not as the recent value of the preceding year's target path. This convention—sometimes called base drift—receives surprisingly little comment given that it can be tantamount to a major quantitative change in the target path.

As an illustration, consider the target cone for M1 for calendar 1981 (see figure 4-1). In its public statements about the target in February 1981, the Federal Reserve emphasized the one-half point reduction in its 1981 target growth ranges for the shift-adjusted measure of this aggregate. In fact, the upward base drift (1.8 percent of the outstanding level of the midpoint of the target cone in the fourth quarter of 1980) was large enough to more than offset the one-half point reduction in the target growth rate. The Federal Reserve can thus be said to have raised rather than lowered its 1981 target path for (shift-adjusted) M1.[3]

The third element of flexibility in the Federal Reserve's use of the intermediate-target strategy is its specification of target cones for several monetary aggregates rather than one alone. The existence of multiple intermediate targets creates substantial scope for discretionary decision-making whenever the various monetary aggregates differ in behavior relative to their target paths.

An especially striking example of such differing behavior occurred throughout most of 1981. By October 1981, M1 was well below the target cone set in early 1981. Yet M2 was right at the top of its target cone (see figure 9-1). Furthermore, M3 was well above the upper boundary of its cone (see figure 9-2).[4] From the policy records of FOMC meetings it is

3. See chap. 4, n. 3, for an explanation of shift-adjusted M1. During 1980 and 1981 the curve for money shown in figures 4-1 and 4-2 was referred to as M1B.

4. M2 is defined as the sum of M1, overnight repurchase agreements at commercial banks, overnight Eurodollars issued by Caribbean branches of member banks to U.S.

Figure 9-1. *M2 Definition of the Money Stock: Actual Path and Target Cones, Fall 1979 through Summer 1982*[a]

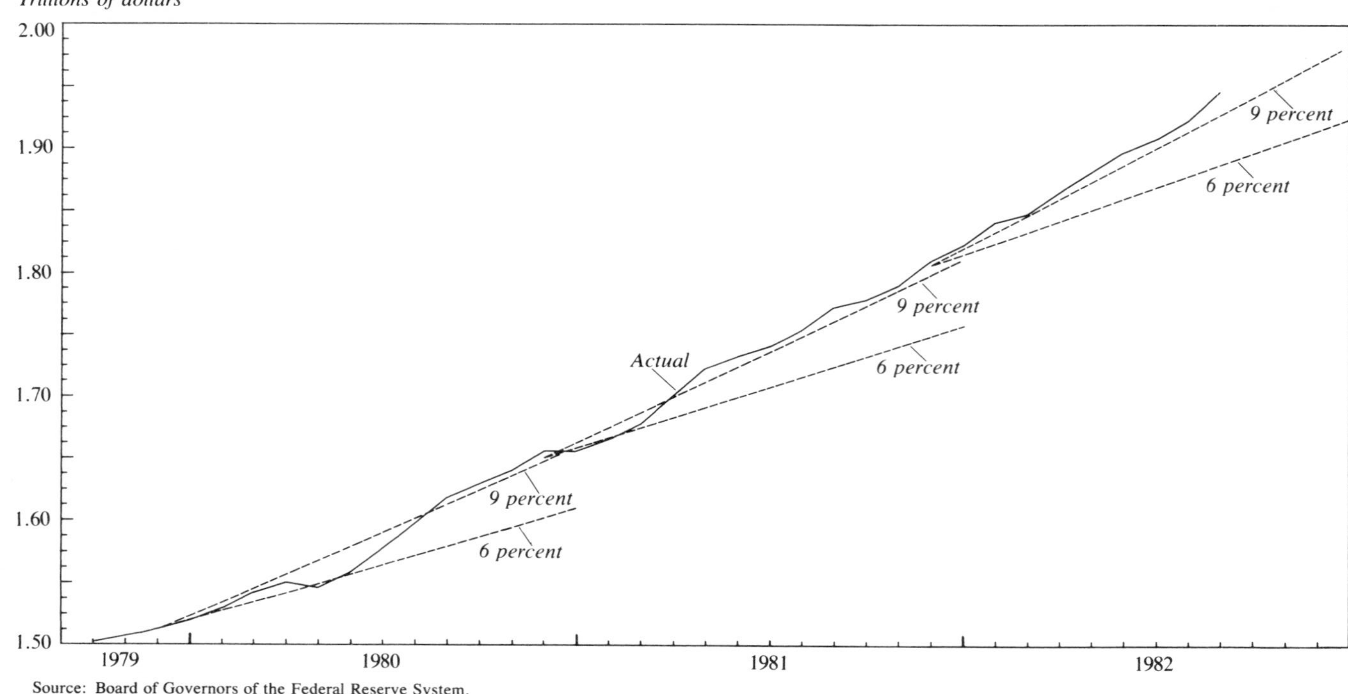

Source: Board of Governors of the Federal Reserve System.
a. Seasonally adjusted monthly averages of daily data.

Figure 9-2. *M3 Definition of the Money Stock: Actual Path and Target Cones, Fall 1979 through Summer 1982*[a]

Trillions of dollars

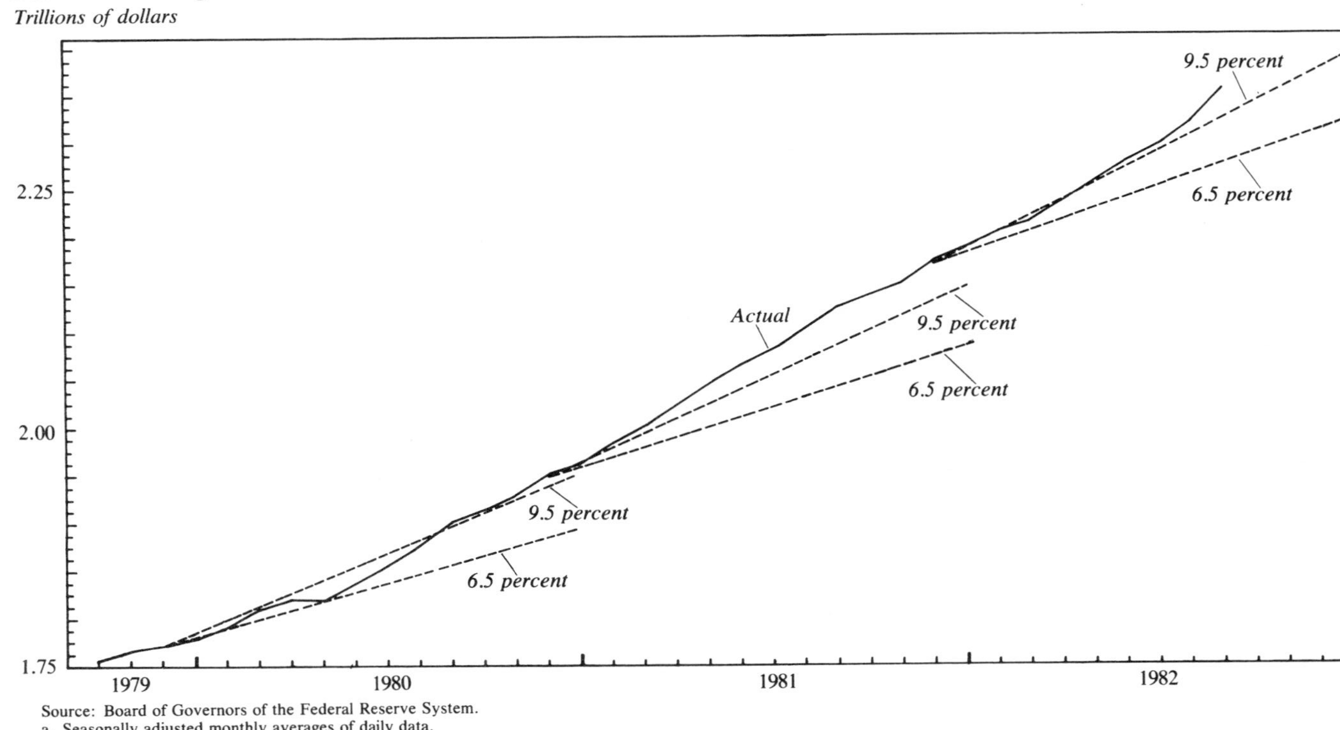

Source: Board of Governors of the Federal Reserve System.

a. Seasonally adjusted monthly averages of daily data.

clear that members of the FOMC sometimes differ among themselves on the weights to be given to the various monetary aggregates. The FOMC as a whole has on occasion deliberately altered these relative weights.

Fourth, the Federal Reserve's response to deviations of money from target has tended to be gradualist rather than aggressive. In several instances the FOMC has deliberately eschewed as rapid a return to path as possible, choosing instead to try to return over a period of several months. This gradualist posture has been characterized as follows by the President of the Federal Reserve Bank of New York:

> We do not feel that it is desirable, or really possible, to control the growth of the monetary aggregates that we are targeting from week to week, month to month, or even necessarily from quarter to quarter. There are a whole host of seasonal factors and other transient influences causing erratic shifts in money demand, and I doubt there is any degree of interest rate movement that could offset these influences over short periods of time and leave money growth on some smooth, steady path.
>
> Therefore, we don't intend or seek to correct deviations in money growth from our long-term targets immediately. We have generally decided to make the corrections over time.[5]

Fifth, the Federal Reserve has at times allowed other considerations to override deviations of the monetary aggregates from target paths. Several examples of this behavior are explicitly described in Federal Reserve documents. One such instance occurred in May 1980. Despite a large shortfall of M1 relative to target path and clear weakness in M2

---

residents other than depository institutions and money market mutual funds, balances held in general-purpose and broker-dealer money market mutual funds, and savings and small denomination time deposits (amounts less than $100,000) issued by commercial banks and thrift institutions. M3 is defined as the sum of M2, large denomination time deposits at commercial banks and thrift institutions (excluding those held by financial institutions and the U.S. government), term repurchase agreements at commercial banks and thrift institutions, and balances held in institution-only money market mutual funds. For discussion of the differing behavior of the various monetary aggregates in 1981, see David E. Lindsey, "Nonborrowed Reserve Targeting and Monetary Control," in Lawrence Meyer, ed., *Improving Money Stock Control: Problems, Solutions, and Consequences* (Federal Reserve Bank of St. Louis, 1982); and Peter D. Sternlight and others, "Monetary Policy and Open Market Operations in 1980."

5. Anthony M. Solomon, "International Coordination of Economic Policies," David Horowitz Lectures of 1982 delivered at the Hebrew University of Jerusalem, March 5, 1982, p. 60. For additional evidence on this point, see Sternlight and others, "Monetary Policy and Open Market Operations in 1980" and "Monetary Policy and Open Market Operations in 1981," and Peter A. Tinsley and others, "Money Market Impacts of Alternative Operating Procedures," in *New Monetary Control Procedures,* vol. 2.

and M3, the FOMC in the latter part of May drained reserves from the banking system to mitigate the sharp fall in short-term interest rates that was then occurring. As explained by the operating officials at the Federal Reserve Bank of New York,

> A further drop in [short-term interest] rates would risk exacerbating inflationary expectations, threatening the value of the dollar in exchange markets, and ultimately requiring a sharp rise in rates later in the year as money growth responded with a lag to the low rates.[6]

To an extent that is of course unclear from the available documents, probably all members of the FOMC occasionally give some weight to information about economic variables other than the money stock when deciding how to vote at meetings. The individual FOMC members least enamored with money targeting undoubtedly give substantial weight to other considerations more or less continuously.

The October 1979 Change in Operating Procedures and Its Significance

Some recent criticism of the Federal Reserve questions the importance of the October 1979 change in operating procedures. It is asserted that the Federal Reserve has not really changed its behavior very much because it still systematically inhibits movements of the federal funds rate, much as it did before October 1979. According to this criticism, episodes like the one in May 1980 referred to above are numerous if not routine rather than the infrequent exception.[7]

I believe this line of criticism is incorrect and misleading. Although often misinterpreted, the October 1979 decision did constitute a major change in the day-to-day conduct of open-market operations.

Figure 9-3 provides presumptive, though not conclusive, evidence on this question. When the Federal Reserve was conducting policy with the

6. Peter Sternlight and others, "Monetary Policy and Open Market Operations in 1980," p. 72.

7. For examples, see Allan H. Meltzer, "Consequences of the Federal Reserve's Re-attachment to Free Reserves," paper presented at the 1981 annual meeting of the Western Economic Association (revised October 1981); and William Poole, "Federal Reserve Operating Procedures: A Survey and Evaluation of the Historical Record Since October 1979," *Journal of Money, Credit and Banking*, vol. 14 (November 1982), pt. 2, pp. 575–96.

Figure 9-3. *Federal Funds Rate: Actual Path and Federal Open Market*

Percent per year

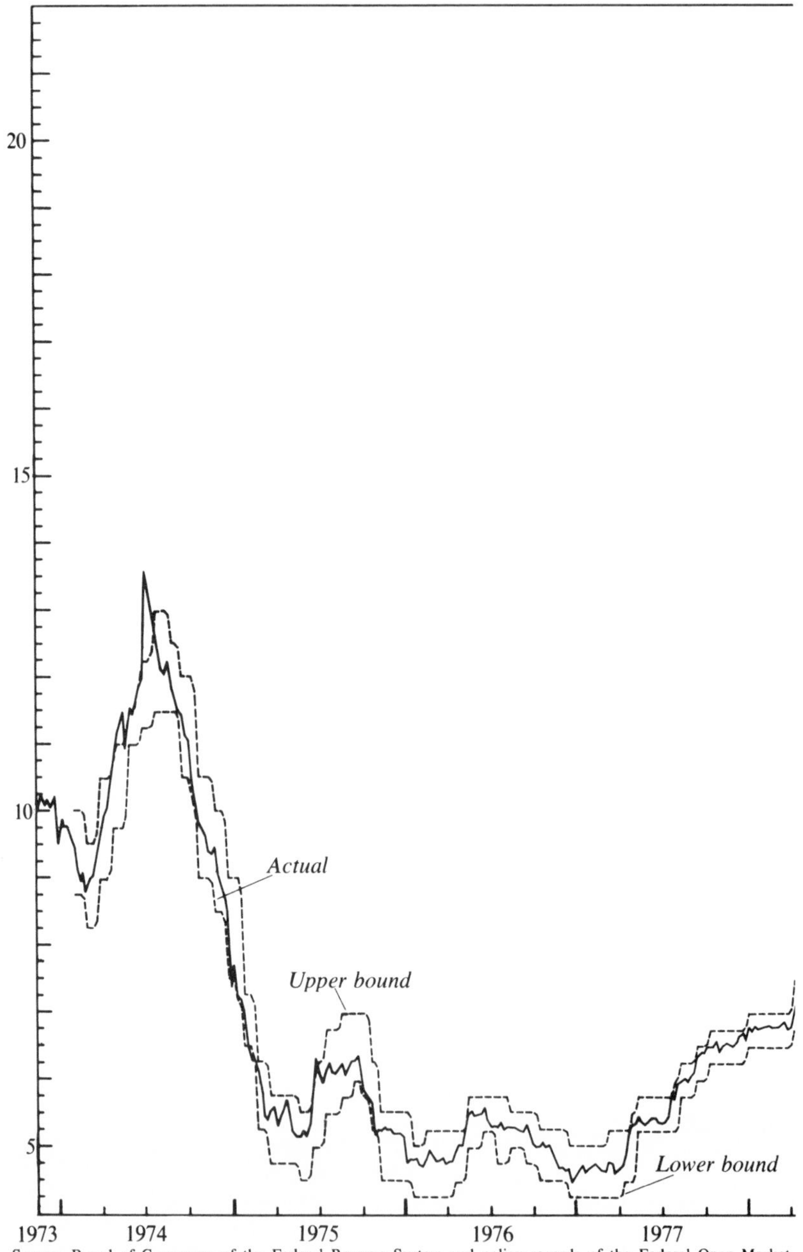

Source: Board of Governors of the Federal Reserve System and policy records of the Federal Open Market Committee.

a. Weekly averages of daily data, not seasonally adjusted.

Committee Constraint, Weekly Data, Fall 1973 through Summer 1982[a]

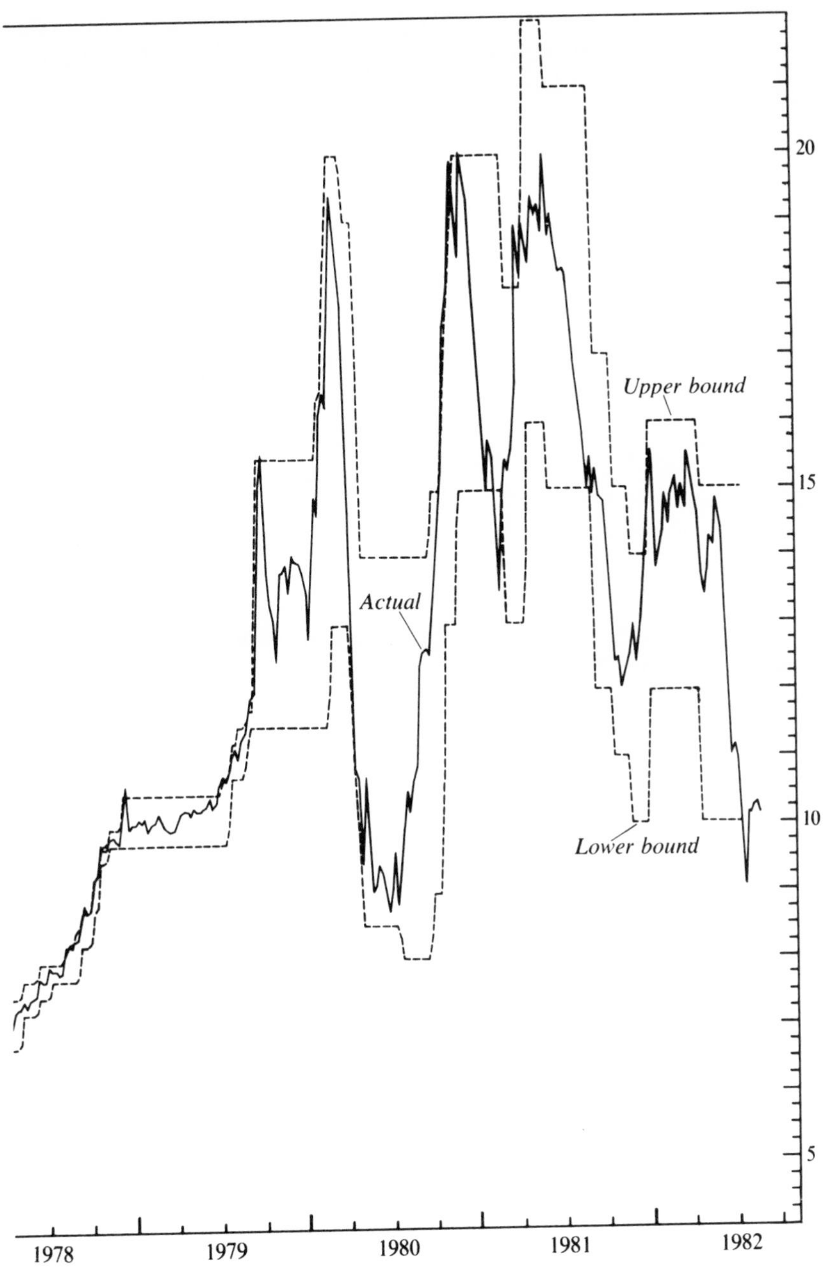

funds-rate regime before October 1979, the FOMC specified at each meeting a range for the federal funds rate; the rate was not permitted to move outside these boundaries in the following weeks. This range, known as the intermeeting funds-rate constraint, was quite narrow (seldom more than 100 basis points and sometimes as few as 50 or 75 points). With the switch to the unborrowed-reserves regime in October 1979, this constraint was necessarily widened a great deal (to at least 400 basis points, and at some times even to 600 points). This change is dramatically evident in the contrast between the left-hand and right-hand portions of figure 9-3.

As is clear from chapter 2, a total-reserves regime would probably have generated still larger fluctuations in the funds rate than those shown in figure 9-3. A more rigid pursuit of the money target paths would probably also have produced even wider swings in interest rates. Given the large nonpolicy disturbances affecting the economy in 1980–82, interest rates would undoubtedly have fluctuated more than in past years even if the Federal Reserve had continued to conduct policy with the funds-rate regime. Those valid points notwithstanding, it strains credulity beyond the breaking point to imagine that a 1980–82 path for the funds rate similar to that in figure 9-3 could have been generated under the operating procedures in use before October 1979.

When the funds rate approached the upper or lower boundary of its constraint after October 1979, the boundary tended to be changed fairly promptly—with greater alacrity, in my opinion, than in previous years. Even more important, however, the existence of the greatly widened constraint permitted market pressures to move the funds rate notably faster and further, toward a boundary but still within the constraint, than was possible before October 1979.

A prominent characteristic of a quantity operating regime is that it permits prompt, substantial changes of the funds rate without necessitating an explicit decision to that effect by the FOMC. In part because of that characteristic, the Federal Reserve has inhibited changes in the funds rate in 1980–82 markedly less than it would have under the former procedures.

Since the October 1979 changes, the trading desk at the Federal Reserve Bank of New York has tended to concentrate its transactions for the day in a forty-five minute period in the middle of the day. In the period between October 1979 and early 1981, the average volume of repurchase agreements and matched sale-purchase transactions was significantly smaller than it had been before the change.[8] Facts such as these are further evidence of the substantial differences between operating procedures before and after October 1979.

It is not yet widely appreciated, furthermore, that the FOMC weakened the significance of the funds-rate constraint still further as 1980 and 1981 progressed. Before October 1979 the upper and lower limits of the constraint were strictly binding day by day (with a temporary exception for Wednesdays at the end of the banking week or for a day subject to highly unusual market pressures). After October 1979, the constraint was interpreted as referring only to the weekly average of the funds rate. In two special telephone meetings in early December 1980, the upper limit of the constraint was suspended rather than, as on analogous occasions in the past, explicitly altered. In the policy record for the regularly scheduled meeting held on December 18–19, 1980, the FOMC directive for the first time used the phrase "taken over a period of time" in referring to the funds-rate constraint. In March 1981 the funds rate was permitted to fall well below the lower limit of the constraint and to stay there for an extended period of several weeks without any explicit FOMC action. Finally, the new flexibility in interpretation of the constraint was explicitly codified in the policy record for the FOMC meeting held on March 31, 1981:

> With respect to the federal funds rate, it was stressed that the Committee specified an intermeeting range for fluctuations over a period of time to provide a mechanism for initiating timely consultations between regularly scheduled meetings whenever it appeared that fluctuations within the specified range were proving to be inconsistent with the objectives for the behavior of reserve and monetary aggregates. Thus, the limits of the range were indicative of the conditions under which the Committee would wish to consult to reexamine its short-run objectives and were not intended as binding constraints on System operations pending such consultations.[9]

The Least Undesirable Way to Implement the Constraints of a Money Strategy

Although on the basis of economic logic an intermediate-target strategy is an inferior approach to the conduct of monetary policy, the Federal Reserve is politically committed to such a strategy.

8. See Fred Levin and Paul Meek, "Implementing the New Procedures: The View from the Trading Desk," in *New Monetary Control Procedures*, vol. 1, pp. 17, 18.

9. Board of Governors of the Federal Reserve System, *68th Annual Report, 1981*, pp. 102–03.

Some form of money targeting is now required by law. The Full Employment and Balanced Growth Act of 1978 amended the Federal Reserve Act, obligating the Federal Reserve twice a year to transmit to the Congress:

> the objectives and plans of the Board of Governors and the Federal Open Market Committee with respect to the ranges of growth or diminution of the monetary and credit aggregates.[10]

Equally important, the Federal Reserve has strongly committed itself to money targeting in its public statements. Especially since the later 1970s, most speeches and congressional testimonies by Federal Reserve officials have encouraged the belief that firm adherence to money targets is the only effective way to reduce inflation. The public statements of President Reagan's administration in 1981 and 1982 about the proper way to conduct monetary policy have zealously embraced this belief.

The political reality, therefore, is that the Federal Reserve is boxed in. At least for the next year or two, it will not be feasible to formulate monetary policy without an emphasis on the money stock as an intermediate target. To be more precise, the Federal Reserve will not be able to describe monetary policy to outsiders without announcing money targets and demonstrating that reasonable efforts are being made to achieve those targets.

What is the least undesirable way to conduct a money strategy given that the Federal Reserve and the administration are politically committed to it? My view is that the existing elements of flexibility in the approach need to be expanded and a better explanation about them given to the general public. Notwithstanding possible urgings by some members of President Reagan's administration, the Federal Reserve should certainly not go in the opposite direction, adhering more closely to a purist variant of the strategy.

Even more than in the recent past, the Federal Reserve should avoid focusing its own and the public's attention on a single monetary target. Specifying target paths for several intermediate variables is, of course, confusing. It is potentially confusing for the FOMC itself if members of the committee slip inadvertently into treating the money targets as reliable surrogates for the ultimate targets of policy. Multiple targets are certainly confusing for the general public, who have been encouraged to

10. 92 Stat. 1897. This language was modeled on the text of U.S. House Concurrent Resolution 133 (89 Stat. 1194), approved in March 1975 by the House and the Senate.

believe that a sound rationale exists for a purist variant of the money strategy.

It is a disservice to the public, however, to pretend that a simple nostrum will resolve a complex, continually changing problem. The real confusion stems from the genuine difficulties facing the U.S. economy and the world economy and, to a lesser extent, from the inherent defects of an intermediate-target strategy. The best route to greater public understanding and credibility for the Federal Reserve is to pursue an economically sound policy and to explain it well. The fact that a nostrum lends itself easily to simple explanation is scarcely a sufficient reason for adopting it. In one sense, it is essentially *constructive* for the general public to be confused by multiple monetary aggregates, especially when the different aggregates behave in nonparallel ways (recall again the very divergent experience of different definitions of money during 1981). Education of the public is, virtually by definition, fostering confusion but at a higher level than before.

In any case, the potential dangers of inflexible commitment to a target path for a single aggregate are sufficient grounds for rejecting that approach. The fundamental point is that deviations of money from a prespecified target path are sometimes undesirable, but sometimes not (see chapters 2 and 3). If target paths for several different aggregates are specified, it is more likely that discretionary judgment will be able to avert instances in which money is wrongly pushed back toward a target path that is no longer appropriate.

Better still, so long as the Federal Reserve is politically committed to adhere to intermediate-target variables, it would be preferable to broaden the menu of such variables beyond the conventional money definitions. Several analysts of monetary policy, for example, have argued that the Federal Reserve should use a "money" aggregate and a "credit" aggregate as targets rather than several money aggregates.[11] They emphasize, correctly, that credit quantities contain important information about the economy that is additional to the information yielded by money quantities. The two types of aggregates provide something of a cross-check on each other, and the Federal Reserve would thus be better off with both as targets than with either one alone.

11. See Benjamin M. Friedman, "The Roles of Money and Credit in Macroeconomic Analysis," in James Tobin, ed., *Macroeconomics, Prices and Quantities: Essays in Memory of Arthur M. Okun* (Brookings Institution, 1983).

To conduct a money strategy so as to minimize its risks, the Federal Reserve should also maintain as much flexibility as it now has in varying the speed with which it attempts to return the aggregates to target paths. For most circumstances, either extreme choice about the speed of reentry—trying to return to the target path within just a few weeks or making an adjustment only very sluggishly—is likely to be incorrect. Aiming to return to the path over a horizon of three to five months might be a judicious compromise, applicable to most circumstances. Instances can arise, however, in which a faster or slower return—or no return at all—would be more appropriate. No rule of thumb about the speed of reentry should be elevated to the status of a maxim.

A similar point applies to the range for the federal funds rate specified at each FOMC meeting. The current practice of interpreting the funds-rate constraint flexibly—as merely a trigger for consultations—is desirable, both in its own right and as an accompaniment to the least unsatisfactory way of conducting a money strategy. Even with the constraint as wide as 500 to 600 basis points, no important purpose would be served by rigid observance of the upper and lower limits. Conversely, if circumstances appear to warrant such action, the Federal Reserve should not hesitate to change its instrument setting for unborrowed reserves to lessen or prevent variations in the funds rate *within* the constraint. Large unexpected variations in that rate may provide important information about new disturbances affecting the economy. A rigid policy in pursuing a hands-off approach when the funds rate is not close to one of its limits can be just as harmful to the economy as a rigid policy of inhibiting the rate from going beyond the limits.

Finally, to conduct a money strategy in a way that yields some of the benefits claimed for it without incurring its greatest disadvantages, the Federal Reserve should continuously reevaluate the reasonableness of the target paths themselves and be willing to adjust them promptly if incoming information and projections warrant a change. Altering the paths requires a careful public explanation of why the changes are desirable. Any upward adjustment will be particularly difficult to explain so long as the price level continues to rise rapidly. But adjustments, down or up, may well be desirable, and not merely on the semiannual occasions when formal FOMC procedures provide for a review of the paths. Note again that the necessity of justifying policy changes to the public, in particular a discretionary change in the money paths, is an opportunity as well as a burden. Each such occasion provides a chance to better educate the public about the role that the money paths should (and should not) play in policy decisions.[12]

Deviations of Money from Target in 1980–82

Throughout the three years beginning in October 1979, and to a greater extent than in previous years, the Federal Reserve tried to restrain growth of the monetary aggregates within the boundaries of its long-run target cones. That effort should be judged a success if one is willing to evaluate performance for the 1980–82 period as a whole and to focus on M1 as the most relevant measure of money.

The grounds for this judgment are apparent in figure 9-4, which shows the time paths for 1980–82 of two measures of M1, the standard definition (the series shown in figure 4-1) and a variant of the so-called shift-adjusted definition. Shift-adjusted M1 differs from standard M1 by an estimate of one-time shifts during 1981 into NOW accounts out of savings deposits not included in M1.[13] Figure 9-4 also shows two dashed lines representing compound rates of growth of 4 and 6.5 percent a year from the average of actual M1 in the fourth quarter of 1979.[14] For the period

12. Nothing in the statutory obligations governing the Federal Reserve—in particular, in the 1978 amendment to the Federal Reserve Act—prohibits the Federal Reserve from adopting the degree of flexibility in money targeting advocated here. In fact, the 1978 amendment also states that "nothing in this act shall be interpreted to require that the objectives and plans with respect to the ranges of growth or diminution of the monetary and credit aggregates disclosed in the reports submitted under this section be achieved if the Board of Governors and the Federal Open Market Committee determine they cannot or should not be achieved because of changing conditions."

13. The 1981 shifts into NOW accounts were triggered by a regulatory change in January 1981 that permitted depository institutions throughout the nation, not merely those in New England, to offer this type of account. The amount of the shift adjustment in 1981 and 1982 (the difference between the two curves in the figure) is a rough estimate by the author, based on published estimates by the Federal Reserve in its H.6 statistical release. The Federal Reserve ceased publication of a shift-adjusted measure in January 1982. My estimates use the Federal Reserve's figures for 1981; to obtain estimates for 1982, I have extrapolated the amount of the Federal Reserve's adjustment for the month of December 1981 ($12.5 billion) and mechanically subtracted that constant amount from the standard M1 measure. A more careful estimate for the months of 1982 would result in a marginally larger adjustment, and hence an estimate of shift-adjusted M1 for 1982 somewhat lower than the curve shown in figure 9-4.

14. For the twelve months from the fourth quarter of 1979 to the fourth quarter of 1980, these dashed lines correspond exactly to the FOMC's target cone (see figure 4-1).

Figure 9-4. *Growth of the Money Stock, M1 Definition, Fall 1979 through Summer 1982*[a]

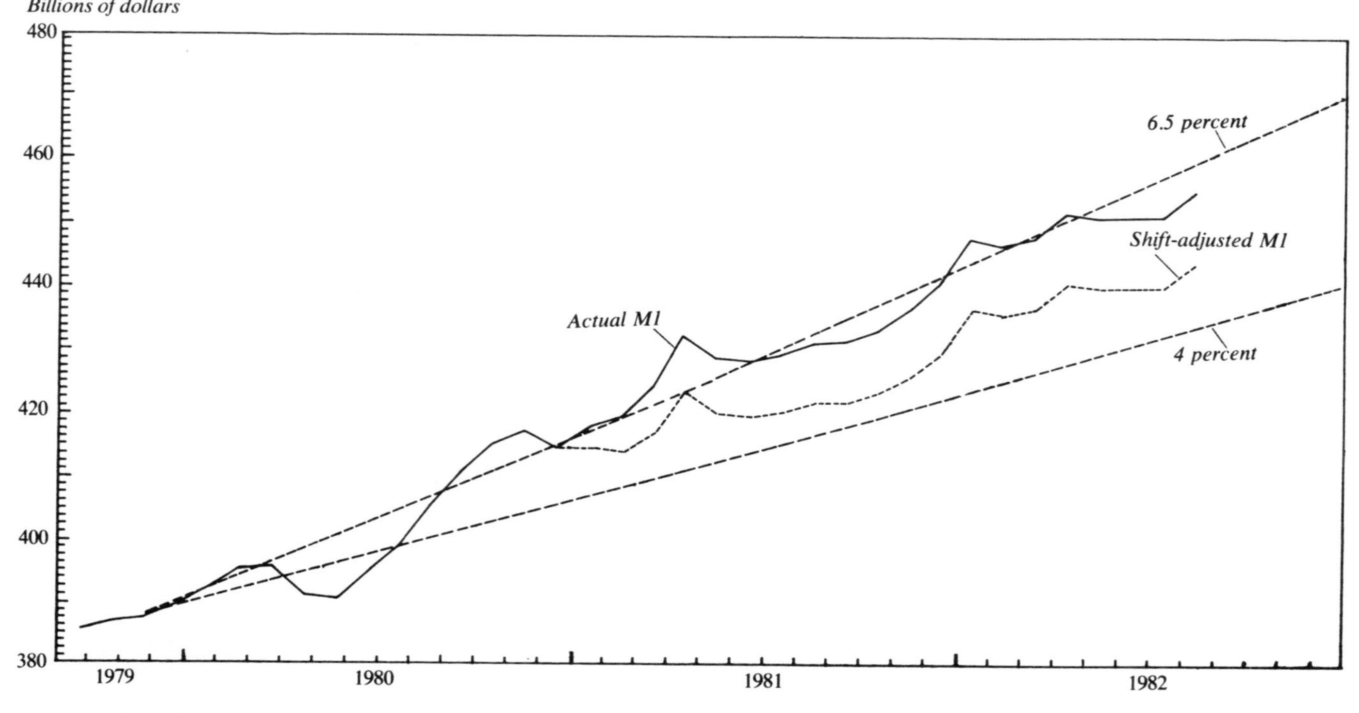

Source: Board of Governors of the Federal Reserve System.
a. Seasonally adjusted monthly averages of daily data. See note 13 for a description of the series for shift-adjusted M1.

shown, M1 grew at a compound annual rate of 5.9 percent and shift-adjusted M1 grew at a rate of only 4.9 percent. These long-run rates of growth, especially if one focuses on the latter figure to allow for the unusual increase in 1981 in NOW accounts, are consistent with the targets set by the FOMC.

An evaluation of the Federal Reserve's performance in restraining the long-run growth of the monetary aggregates is not quite so straightforward if attention is focused on the M2 and M3 definitions of money. As can be seen in figures 9-1 and 9-2, those two measures have grown at rates near the top of or above the FOMC's target cones. Even for those measures, however, long-run growth has been relatively moderate and not dramatically greater than the Federal Reserve's targets. (For the period shown in those figures, M2 grew at a compound annual rate of 9.3 percent and M3 grew at a rate of 10.6 percent.)

Between fall 1979 and late summer 1982 the Federal Reserve and the public both gave primary emphasis to the M1 measure of money. To evaluate the performance of the Federal Reserve in achieving money targets, therefore, figure 9-4 is more relevant than figures 9-1 and 9-2.[15]

On the basis of the 1980–82 experience, pragmatic monetarists have little basis for criticizing the Federal Reserve for its implementation of a money-targeting strategy. (Pragmatic monetarists, it will be recalled from chapter 7, are those who advocate averaging control of the money stock over a medium- or long-run period.) The average level of M1 over the three-year period was not far from the average value of the successive annual target paths (in particular, for shift-adjusted M1). The shortfall in spring 1980 was roughly counterbalanced by the overshoot in fall 1980. The weakness in mid-1981 was partially offset by strength in early 1982. All things considered, therefore, pragmatic monetarists ought to argue that the Federal Reserve performed well in achieving its long-run money targets.

Some critics of the Federal Reserve have been preoccupied with the month-to-month and quarter-to-quarter fluctuations in M1 that are evident in figure 9-4. They interpret those fluctuations as evidence that the Federal Reserve failed to control M1 appropriately. For reasons fully discussed in chapters 4 through 6, complaints from such critics about the 1980–82 performance of the Federal Reserve in controlling money can justifiably be discounted.

15. See note 4 at the beginning of this chapter for references that discuss the reasons for the divergent behavior of the narrow and broad monetary aggregates in 1981–82.

If complaints from monetarists about the implementation of the money-targeting procedure have a weak foundation, two other types of criticism of the Federal Reserve's policy in 1980–82 rest on firmer ground. Arguments of the first type—asserting that the money-targeting procedure, however implemented, is an inherently inferior approach for conducting monetary policy—have already been summarized in chapter 8 and will not be elaborated further here. Criticisms of the second type question the appropriateness of the numerical values of the long-run money targets set by the Federal Reserve. This latter line of criticism extends the debate about Federal Reserve performance beyond the issue of whether a money-targeting procedure is an acceptable method for implementing monetary policy. Criticisms of the quantitative values of the targets can be made from either a monetarist or a nonmonetarist perspective.

The 1980–82 Money Targets as Part of Overall Macroeconomic Policy

Whether the numerical values of the money targets in 1980–82 were appropriate for the American economy is a more important question about Federal Reserve performance than any issue considered up to this point. It is also an extremely difficult question, requiring analysis of topics that have not even been broached, much less examined, in the preceding pages.

Indeed, the numerical values of the money targets cannot be evaluated without analyzing the macroeconomic policies of the U.S. government in their entirety. The overall objectives of economic policy—for example, the importance assigned to reducing inflation relative to the importance of maintaining employment at a high level—are centrally relevant to an evaluation of the money targets. So, too, is an assessment of the mix of monetary policy and fiscal policy, and of fiscal policy itself. The president, his administration, and Congress—at least as much as the Federal Reserve—establish the overall objectives of the nation's economic policies. Decisions about the numerical values of the money targets and other aspects of monetary policy cannot be sensibly evaluated in isolation from decisions about tax revenues, expenditures, and transfer payments in the government's budget.

In contrast to the preceding statement, in the 1950s and 1960s some knowledgeable economists believed, or seemed to believe, that fiscal policy matters so little for the macroeconomic evolution of the economy that specification of money targets can safely ignore fiscal actions. Today, however, knowledgeable differences of view about the relative importance of monetary policy and fiscal policy turn on the magnitudes and timing patterns of the impacts of the two types of policy actions, not on whether one or the other can be ignored altogether. To be sure, the view that money targets can be specified without regard to the current and prospective stance of fiscal policy has a strong political attraction for individuals who for quite separate reasons wish to pretend that the macroeconomic effects of fiscal actions can be de-emphasized or forgotten. But that view does not merit attention in a serious analysis of the least inappropriate way to specify money targets.[16]

My personal views about the overriding issues of macroeconomic policy in recent years are critical of the Federal Reserve, Congress, and the administration. I believe that the policy goal of reducing inflation was pursued too zealously in 1980–82 in the United States without sufficient regard for the probable costs in unemployment and lost output. Even if that paramount emphasis on reducing inflation is accepted as given, moreover, I believe that the mix of monetary policy and fiscal policy in the United States was seriously wrong in 1980–82. The American economy would have been better served with more fiscal restraint (in particular, *prospective* restraint in the federal government's budget for the middle and late years of the 1980s) offset by somewhat higher target paths for money. The American people would certainly have been better served with more realistic projections from President Reagan's administration about the budgetary consequences of large tax reductions and vigorous expansion in defense spending combined with restrained growth in money.

To provide a careful analysis of overall U.S. macroeconomic policies

16. The late Arthur Okun, writing over twelve years ago, commented on 1960s-vintage proposals for conducting monetary policy with a rule for the growth in the money stock. "What is most important and most dangerous about the monetary rule," noted Okun, "is its implicit precept: ignore fiscal policy. . . . Carried to its ultimate conclusions, the monetarist position would justify a totally unconstrained federal fiscal policy. Now I know a few people in Washington who would love an intellectual justification for fiscal irresponsibility. Some day they are going to discover the most important message of the monetarist view. And then we will see some fireworks." See *The Political Economy of Prosperity* (Brookings Institution, 1970), pp. 116–17. Okun's observation was proven highly prescient by the policy decisions of the president and Congress in 1981–82.

and to articulate the reasoning behind the personal views in the preceding paragraph are tasks well beyond the scope of this book. I mention here the numerical values of the money targets and the many ramifications of decisions about them to be sure the reader understands that the topics discussed in this chapter are merely a prelude to an in-depth evaluation of the performance of the Federal Reserve in fulfilling its policy responsibilities.

CHAPTER TEN

Concluding Comments

George Orwell wryly observed that the facts are often disregarded by both sides in a debate. There are some people, he pointed out, who will always assume that the bishop has a mistress. There are others who will go to any length to continue believing that the bishop simply regards pastoral care as a twenty-four-hour duty. The traditional debate between monetarists and antimonetarists may be another illustration of these propensities, and hence may always be with us. Yet I still nourish the hope that a dissipation of confusion and a narrowing of disagreement is possible.

Most of this book is an exposition of points that should not be controversial. In particular, I see little reason for continued controversy about alternative Federal Reserve operating regimes and the ability of the Federal Reserve to control the money stock. The analysis summarized in chapters 2 and 3 does not give a laurel wreath to either the traditional monetarist or the traditional antimonetarist position. The best insights economists have about the problem of instrument choice cannot, in fact, be accurately described as either monetarist or antimonetarist. Similarly, what is needed in discussions about the determination of the money stock is a more eclectic perspective, one that acknowledges not only the fundamental role of Federal Reserve policy actions but also the importance of nonpolicy influences.

The arguments against the use of the money stock as a surrogate target, summarized in chapter 8, are controversial. Here too, however, I believe that only limited grounds exist for further debate. If correct, those arguments provide a solid case for rejecting the use of a two-stage money strategy. Those who continue to support such an approach should at least face those arguments squarely and show why they are wrong or inapplicable.

As this book goes to press, the financial system and the real economy in the United States are more than normally fragile. The probability of a spate of nonfinancial bankruptcies and the consequent failure of numerous financial intermediaries, although not large, is nonetheless distressingly high relative to the probability of such events in a healthy economy. Unexpected events, including political turmoil abroad or a deeper and more protracted recession than currently foreseen by most economic forecasters, could raise that probability still further.

If major cracks in the financial system should start to appear and confidence should suddenly weaken, that would be an especially inappropriate time for zealous efforts to achieve prespecified targets for growth in the money stock. The deterioration in confidence could spark a sharp increase in the precautionary demand for liquid assets; a correct response by the Federal Reserve would accommodate those increased demands, despite a resulting increase in the money stock. Both the advocates and the critics of money targeting could, I hope, agree on at least that much. If such an unfortunate contingency should occur, the Federal Reserve will need support from all shades of opinion in the economics profession to explain why sizable, temporary departures from the long-run money targets are highly desirable.

The case against a two-stage money strategy, it should be clear, is not an "anti-money" case. Still less is it "pro-interest rate." When implementing monetary policy, the Federal Reserve does not have to choose, and should not choose, between emphasizing a financial quantity *or* a financial price. The fundamental problem with money targeting is its two-stage decision procedure, not its selection of a financial quantity as the surrogate target. A two-stage strategy using a price variable as the surrogate target (for example, a long-term interest rate) would in many circumstances be even worse than a money strategy.

The genuine issues confronting the Federal Reserve are obscured by identifying them as money versus interest rates or monetarism versus Keynesianism. Monetarists who argue against stabilizing interest rates are correct—some of the time. Keynesians who argue against stabilizing financial quantities are correct—some of the time. The key point, however, is that neither a price-stabilization nor a quantity-stabilization presumption is the appropriate guideline for monetary policy in all circumstances.

No good reason exists for the Federal Reserve to emphasize quantities instead of prices, or prices instead of quantities. Operas require a libretto and a score. A sensible approach to monetary policy requires an integrated perception of both prices and quantities, combined with a differentiation of decisions in accordance with the current and prospective circumstances of the economy.

The truly important issues about the conduct of monetary policy—those most deserving of debate—are either not mentioned in this book at all or else are alluded to only briefly. These issues include rules versus discretion, the relations between monetary policy and fiscal policy, the preferred macroeconomic policies for reducing inflation, and the interdependence of monetary policy in the United States and monetary policies in the rest of the world.

In its traditional form, the rules versus discretion issue is a debate about the pros and cons of insulating monetary policy from the political process, from human incompetence, or both. The issue also has a modern guise as a controversy about expectational, game-theoretic interactions between the private sector and the government (for example, about the "time inconsistency problem" that can arise for discretionary policy). Both forms of the issue are concerned with the appropriate degree of "activism" permitted to policymakers. Both forms are controversial. Both merit extensive further research.[1]

The set of issues concerned with how monetary policy and fiscal policy relate to each other is equally worthy of further research, and even more controversial. Disagreement arises over whether to coordinate monetary policy with fiscal policy, and if so, how. That disagreement stems naturally from controversy about the pros and cons of a politically independent central bank. What is really at stake here is the basic political question of who should choose the ultimate goals to be pursued by the Federal Reserve.

Controversy is rife among policymakers and economists about the most appropriate policies for combating inflation. The disagreements arise partly from differences in social values (for example, the relative weights attached to such ultimate goals of economic policy as low inflation, high employment, and rapid growth in output). Other important factors in the disagreements, however, stem from differences in analytical diagnoses (for example, why rapid inflation can coexist with high

1. Note again, however, that the possible validity of political or game-theoretic arguments against discretionary policy do not obviously justify support for the use of the money stock as a surrogate target. If a valid case exists for conducting monetary policy with a simple rule, the rule will probably have to be specified in terms of an actual instrument of policy.

unemployment). Intense controversy about anti-inflationary policies, both in general and in particular about Federal Reserve policies, is probably inevitable for several years to come. The issues here are genuine and difficult, and little progress toward a consensus can yet be detected.

The international issues, left entirely aside in this book, stem from the growing financial openness of the American economy. When the Federal Reserve takes a policy action, a modest—but an increasingly less modest—part of the effects of the action leaks out to foreign nations. When foreign nations take policy actions or when nonpolicy disturbances originate abroad, an increasingly greater part of the effects spills over into the United States. As a consequence of the growing interdependence of the American economy and the economies of other nations, the policy decisions of the Federal Reserve and of other central banks become more difficult to make and more uncertain in their consequences. At the same time that the American economy experiences growing benefits from interdependence, the ability of U.S. policymakers to achieve national objectives is undermined. These developments in turn suggest that the Federal Reserve and the administration will be forced with increasing frequency to confront the difficulties and potentialities of international cooperation, including the promotion of international institutions that can catalyze that cooperation. In essence the issues of collective action that have been confronted within the United States, or in many cases are still being confronted, will progressively have to be confronted on an international scale.

With such difficult issues as these to analyze, monetary economists, political scientists, and social theorists—not to mention policymakers themselves—should put the older, now sterile debates about monetarism and Keynesianism behind them and get on with higher priority matters that genuinely command attention.

APPENDIX A

A Schematic Framework for the Analysis of Money Supply and Demand

THE SIMPLIFIED FRAMEWORK described here in detail was summarized in chapter 2. This appendix also derives the analytical results presented in tables 2-1 through 2-6.

A schematic description similar in its essentials has been used in several recent papers by Peter Tinsley and his colleagues on the staff of the Federal Reserve Board.[1] The Federal Reserve staff has also estimated a monthly econometric model incorporating the elements of such a framework.[2] A number of earlier papers by other researchers contain expositions along similar lines.[3]

1. See Peter A. Tinsley and others, "Money Market Impacts of Alternative Operating Procedures," in Board of Governors of the Federal Reserve System, *New Monetary Control Procedures*, vol. 2 (The Board, 1981); Peter Tinsley, "A Field Manual for Stochastic Money Market Impacts of Alternative Operating Procedures," unpublished manuscript (Federal Reserve Board, June 1981); memorandum, S. M. Axilrod to the Board, "Contemporaneous Reserve Requirements: A Review of Operational and Monetary Control Considerations," including memorandum, Peter Tinsley and others to the Board, "Estimated Monetary Policy Consequences of Reserve Accounting Procedures," September 14, 1981. See also Michael G. Hadjimichalakis, "Precision of Monetary Control and Volatility of Rates: A Comparative Analysis of the Reserves and the Federal Funds Operating Targets," Special Studies Paper 150 (Federal Reserve Board, Division of Research and Statistics, January 1981).

2. See Helen T. Farr, "The Monthly Money Market Model," staff working paper (Federal Reserve Board of Governors, Econometric and Computer Applications Section, July 1981). For an earlier, published version of the model, see Thomas D. Thomson, James L. Pierce, and Robert T. Parry, "A Monthly Money Market Model," *Journal of Money, Credit and Banking*, vol. 7 (November 1975), pp. 411–31. See also Richard G. Anderson and Robert H. Rasche, "What Do Money Market Models Tell Us about How to Implement Monetary Policy?" *Journal of Money, Credit and Banking*, vol. 14 (November 1982), pt. 2, pp. 796–828; and Helen T. Farr and Richard D. Porter, "Comment on 'What Do Money Market Models Tell Us about How to Implement Policy?' " *Journal of Money, Credit and Banking*, vol. 14 (November 1982), pt. 2, pp. 857–68.

3. For example, see James L. Pierce and Thomas D. Thomson, "Some Issues in

Table A-1. *Schematic Balance Sheet for the U.S. Monetary Authorities*

	Assets
BOR	Borrowed reserves (borrowing by financial intermediaries from the Federal Reserve)
S^{MA}	Security portfolio of the monetary authorities
Flt	Float
OA	Other assets (including tangible assets)
	Liabilities and capital accounts
CUR	Currency in circulation
RT	Total reserves (deposits of financial intermediaries held at the Federal Reserve)
RR	Reserves required against the deposit liabilities of the financial intermediaries
RX	Excess reserves
Dep^{G}	Deposit balance of the government with the Federal Reserve
NW^{MA}	Surplus and capital accounts (net worth)

Basic Elements of an Analytical Framework

Table A-1 presents a schematic balance sheet for the monetary authorities in the United States. This balance sheet is a consolidation of the Federal Reserve balance sheet and certain monetary accounts of the U.S. Treasury.[4] Counterpart balance sheets for the consolidated sector of private financial intermediaries and for the private nonbank sector are shown in tables A-2 and A-3.

This framework postulates only one type of private financial intermediary—henceforth "banks." These banks issue only one type of deposit, *D*. Banks are required to hold a fraction of their deposit liabilities in the form of deposits that do not bear interest at the Federal Reserve (required reserves, *RR*). Deposits of banks at the Federal Reserve above

Controlling the Stock of Money," in Federal Reserve Bank of Boston Conference Series No. 9, *Controlling the Monetary Aggregates II: The Implementation* (Federal Reserve Bank of Boston, 1973), pp. 115–36.

4. A consolidation of the Federal Reserve and these accounts of the Treasury is required to acknowledge the fact that a small part of the currency in circulation in the United States is a liability of the Treasury rather than the Federal Reserve System. (When international aspects of the U.S. monetary system are taken into account, a consolidation is also necessary because the Treasury rather than the Federal Reserve holds most of U.S. international reserve assets.)

Table A-2. *Schematic Consolidated Balance Sheet for Financial Intermediaries*

	Assets
RR	Required reserves held against deposit liabilities
RX	Excess reserves
S^B	Securities
L	Loans to nonbanks
TA^B	Tangible assets
	Liabilities and capital accounts
RB	Borrowed reserves
Flt	Float
D	Deposits of nonbanks
NW^B	Surplus and capital accounts (net worth)[a]

a. The net worth of financial intermediaries is an asset from the perspective of the nonbank sector (included in TA^N in table A-3).

Table A-3. *Schematic Consolidated Balance Sheet for All Nonbanks in the Private Sector*[a]

	Assets
CUR	Currency
D	Deposit claims on financial intermediaries
S^N	Securities
TA^N	Tangible assets and other claims[b]
	Liabilities and net worth
L	Loans from financial intermediaries
NW^N	Net worth of the nonbank sector

a. All nonbank economic units are aggregated in this schematic balance sheet; the claims and liabilities that link households and firms are thus washed out in the consolidation.
b. Includes equity claims on financial intermediaries (NW^B in table A-2).

the required amount are excess reserves, *RX*. Currency, *CUR*, is assumed to be held only by the nonbank private sector.[5]

Banks are permitted to borrow at the Federal Reserve discount window, paying interest at the discount rate, r^d. Given the level at which the Federal Reserve sets the discount rate and given the other regulations for using the window, the amount of this borrowing, *BOR*, is assumed to be determined by the banks. The proximate effect of an increase or

5. In practice, banks maintain a modest inventory of currency ("vault cash") and are permitted to count these currency holdings as part of required reserves. None of the analytical points stressed in this book would be altered if banks' holdings of vault cash were explicitly included in the schematic framework.

decrease in BOR is to increase or decrease RX (and hence also total reserves, RT) by an equivalent amount.

Float, Flt, is a financial magnitude generated by timing discrepancies in the payments mechanism.[6] As checks are processed and collected in the payments system, the Federal Reserve tends on average to credit the reserve accounts of receiving banks sooner than it debits the reserve accounts of paying banks. Float is thus a net asset item on the balance sheet of the Federal Reserve and a net liability item on the balance sheet of the banks. The size of the float item changes by large amounts from week to week. The proximate effect of an increase in float is to increase RX and RT by equivalent amounts.

Changes in the deposit balance at the Federal Reserve of the government, Dep^G, have proximate effects on bank reserves opposite to those of changes in float. For example, an increase in Dep^G reduces RX and RT by an equivalent amount.

Two items on the balance sheet of the monetary authorities—other assets, OA, and the "net worth" account, NW^{MA}—change little if at all from one short-run period to the next and have little significance for the conduct of monetary policy. These accounts are ignored here.

Written in first-difference form, the balance-sheet identity of the monetary authorities in this schematic framework is thus

$$\text{(A-1)} \quad \Delta BOR + \Delta S^{MA} + \Delta Flt - \Delta CUR - \Delta RT - \Delta Dep^G \equiv 0.$$

Just as the balance-sheet identity of the Federal Reserve is a strait-jacket confining the real-life conduct of monetary policy, the identity A-1 plays a central role in this analytical framework.

The total of banks' deposits at the Federal Reserve (total reserves) is the sum of required and excess reserves:

$$\text{(A-2)} \qquad \Delta RT \equiv \Delta RR + \Delta RX.$$

Unborrowed reserves, RU, are defined as total reserves less the banks' borrowing at the discount window:

$$\text{(A-3)} \qquad \Delta RU \equiv \Delta RT - \Delta BOR.$$

The monetary base, B, is the sum of total reserves and currency in circulation:

$$\text{(A-4)} \qquad \Delta B \equiv \Delta RT + \Delta CUR.$$

6. See Benjamin Wolkowitz and Peter R. Lloyd-Davies, "Reducing Federal Reserve Float," *Federal Reserve Bulletin*, vol. 65 (December 1979), pp. 945–50.

The behavior of the banks in borrowing from the Federal Reserve can be represented in highly simplified form as

$$\Delta BOR = c(\Delta r^{ff} - \Delta r^{d}) + \Delta u_{BR}; \qquad c > 0. \tag{A-5}$$

Given the discount rate set by the Federal Reserve, the banks borrow increasingly large amounts at the discount window as the federal funds rate, r^{ff}, rises above the discount rate. The stochastic term, u_{BR}, represents all the factors other than the spread between r^{ff} and r^{d} that determine borrowing. In real life, when r^{ff} falls below r^{d}, *BOR* decreases to low "frictional" levels; however, *BOR* cannot be negative. Less simplified representations of an equation for *BOR* take this point into account and also introduce other determinants such as a bank scale variable and measures of deposit variability (for further discussion see appendix B and the references given there).

The banks' required reserves are the product of the reserve-requirement ratio, h, and reservable deposits, D. Because only one type of deposit is considered in this schematic framework, no scope exists for changes in required reserves due to shifts among types of deposit. In real life, shifts among types of deposit and shifts of deposits among banks of different sizes do give rise to unpredictable changes in required reserves. Furthermore, when making ex ante projections to guide its policy, the Federal Reserve can make errors in its projections of the amount of deposits against which reserves must be held. To represent this type of slippage in the short-run conduct of monetary policy, the expression for required reserves is written as

$$\Delta RR = h\Delta D + \Delta u_{RR}, \tag{A-6}$$

where u_{RR} represents a stochastic term allowing for changes in *RR* that are not completely predictable ex ante by the Federal Reserve.[7]

The framework here assumes that the banks maintain required reserves against their deposits on a "contemporaneous" basis. Equation A-6 asserts, in other words, that an increase in deposits of one dollar in the current period must result in an increase in required reserves of h dollars, *to be held in the current period*.[8]

7. For a more detailed discussion of modeling the links between deposits and required reserves, see Tinsley and others, "Estimated Monetary Policy Consequences of Reserve Accounting Procedures," September 14, 1981.

8. Following the full implementation of the Monetary Control Act of 1980 (the phase-in period for some depository institutions lasts until 1987), the effective reserve

In the United States beginning in September 1968 the Federal Reserve permitted banks to fulfill their reserve requirements on a "lagged" rather than contemporaneous basis (see chapter 6). The 1968 decision generated considerable controversy, however, and gave rise to a literature discussing the relative merits of lagged and contemporaneous accounting.[9] After extensive debate in the early 1980s, a majority of the members of the Federal Reserve Board eventually decided in the summer of 1982 to restore an essentially contemporaneous reserve-accounting procedure.

I use the assumption of contemporaneous reserve accounting in the exposition here for two related reasons. First, a schematic framework incorporating lagged reserve accounting requires an explicit modeling of different time periods and lagged behavioral responses, thereby rendering the exposition significantly more complex. The basic points I emphasize in chapters 2 and 3 are valid for either lagged or contemporaneous reserve requirements. Since my purpose is to help readers understand those basic points, I avoid a detailed discussion of lagged reserve accounting and its differences from contemporaneous accounting.

My second reason is also tactical. A number of critics of the Federal Reserve allege that lagged reserve requirements have been a major determinant of "erratic" movement of the money stock since 1968. I believe that this view exaggerates the significance of the differences between lagged and contemporaneous accounting (see chapter 6). Here, however, I give the benefit of the doubt to the critics. Because equation A-6 assumes contemporaneous accounting, the analysis in chapters 2 and 3 cannot be rejected on the ground that its reserve-accounting assumptions unfairly bias the conclusions against the view of the critics.

In principle, the excess reserves held by banks depend on the opportunity cost of holding them. In the simplified framework here, one could model this behavior by making the change in excess reserves depend negatively on the change in the federal funds rate as well as on a stochastic disturbance, u_{RX}:

$$\text{(A-7a)} \qquad \Delta RX = d\Delta r^{ff} + \Delta u_{RX}; \qquad d < 0.$$

---

requirement on the first $25 million of transactions balances—demand deposits and other checkable deposits—will be 3 percent and the requirement on deposits above that amount will be 12 percent; the reserve requirement for nonpersonal time deposits with a maturity of less than four years will be 3 percent. In the 1970s and early 1980s, the *average* reserve-requirement ratio on all types of deposits at commercial banks was a relatively small number (the average value of h fell in the range of 0.03 to 0.05).

9. See notes in chapter 6 for references to the literature.

In practice, excess reserves do have a negative interest elasticity; whether this elasticity can be successfully estimated in econometric equations, however, depends on whether the empirical equation also allows for the phenomena of "carry-over" and "as of adjustments," as labeled by the Federal Reserve (see appendix B). For the purposes of a very simplified exposition, it is convenient to assume that the coefficient d in equation A-7a is equal to zero, and hence that the entire amount of the change in excess reserves is not readily predictable by the Federal Reserve. Thus

$$\Delta RX = \Delta u_{RX}. \tag{A-7}$$

The conclusions stressed in chapters 2 through 6 would, if anything, be reinforced by allowing for a nonzero interest elasticity.

Two other behavioral relations are schematically represented in this framework. These constitute the "demand" side of the process determining the money stock:

$$\Delta CUR = a_1 \Delta r^{ff} + b_1 \Delta Y + \Delta u_C; \qquad a_1 < 0,\ b_1 > 0 \tag{A-8}$$

$$\Delta D = a_2 \Delta r^{ff} + b_2 \Delta Y + \Delta u_D; \qquad a_2 < 0,\ b_2 > 0. \tag{A-9}$$

Equation A-8 makes currency demand depend positively on nominal GNP, Y, and negatively on the federal funds rate. Deposit demand in equation A-9 is similarly simplified. The terms u_C and u_D denote stochastic disturbances in the equations—that is, changes in currency demand and deposit demand *not* attributable to variations in the nominal value of activity and in interest rates.[10]

Although not a sophisticated specification of money demand, equations A-8 and A-9 nonetheless contain the two essential behavioral elements common to all specifications—a positive elasticity for nominal activity (as a proxy for transactions) and a negative elasticity for nominal interest rates (as a proxy for the opportunity cost of holding money-like assets that bear little or no interest).

In this schematic framework the money stock itself is the sum of currency and the single type of deposits,

$$\Delta M \equiv \Delta CUR + \Delta D. \tag{A-10}$$

The framework sketched above obviously omits many aspects of the

10. An exogenous increase in currency demand is indicated by $\Delta u_C > 0$, an exogenous increase in deposit demand by $\Delta u_D > 0$, and a shift into currency out of deposits by $\Delta u_C = -\Delta u_D$.

behavior of nonbanks and financial intermediaries that are important in real life. For example, it does not contain a "loan market," with demand and supply functions for loans and hence a loan interest rate, r^L, that is endogenously determined in the framework. It does not allow for a bank scale variable (for example, $D + BOR - RR$) in the equations for BOR and RX. It does not contain an interest-rate variable, r^D, for the interest paid on deposits or a bank behavioral equation for the "supply" of deposits. (Such an equation could, for example, specify how the banks set the rate r^D to obtain the quantity of deposits they want to accept.)[11] The framework does not include behavioral equations for other aspects of nonbank financial behavior; it shows explicitly only the demands for assets deemed to be money. For simplicity, the framework shows only first differences of variables; it thus ignores lagged responses and the complex dynamic effects that they can generate.

More broadly, this framework is limited to the "money market." It does not purport to describe the links between the money market and other financial markets or the many links between financial markets and the real sectors of the economy.

As chapter 2 emphasized, these limitations are severe. The framework is therefore inadequate for analyzing many important questions about the conduct of monetary policy. I use the framework merely as an expositional device to bring out conclusions that would continue to be true in more complex and realistic frameworks.

Alternative Operating Regimes

To use the schematic framework summarized by equations A-1 through A-10 as a model of how supply and demand considerations determine the money stock, one must have in mind a clear classification of variables as exogenous or endogenous. Given the simplifications of the framework, three variables—Y, Flt, and Dep^G—are unambiguously exogenous. These variables cannot be controlled by the Federal Reserve.

11. One rationale for omitting r^D and a bank supply equation for D is that regulation Q sets the nominal interest rate on demand deposits at zero and the nominal interest rate on most types of savings and small time deposits at rates significantly below market-determined rates. As Lindsey emphasizes, however, an increasing proportion, now nearly two-thirds, of the "nontransactions" deposits included in the broader monetary aggregate M2 pays a market-related rate of interest. See David E. Lindsey, "Nonborrowed Reserve Targeting and Monetary Control," in Lawrence Meyer, ed., *Improving Money Stock Control: Problems, Solutions, and Consequences* (Federal Reserve Bank of St. Louis, 1982), pp. 3–41.

Moreover, they are determined by outside factors not taken into account here. Likewise, the five stochastic disturbances—u_{BR}, u_{RR}, u_{RX}, u_C, and u_D—are exogenous forces in the senses that their behavior is determined outside the schematic framework and is not controllable by the Federal Reserve. The discount rate is also an exogenous variable. Unlike the preceding variables, however, r^d is a policy instrument. The Federal Reserve can and does set the value of r^d day by day.

Apart from the variables mentioned in the preceding paragraph, the ten equations in the schematic framework contain eleven other variables. Six of these—*M*, *CUR*, *D*, *BOR*, *RR*, and *RX*—are unambiguously endogenous. The remaining five variables—the "price," r^{ff}, and the four "quantities," S^{MA}, *RT*, *RU*, and *B*—are in a peculiar category. Each of these five could conceivably be used by the Federal Reserve as a policy instrument; in other words, each is *potentially* exogenous. Once the Federal Reserve selects one of the five as an *actual* policy instrument, however, the remaining four become endogenous variables.

The schematic framework becomes an internally consistent model of the processes determining the money stock (ten equations determining ten endogenous variables) once an assumption is made about which one of the five potentially exogenous variables the Federal Reserve actually decides to use as its main policy instrument. To be more precise, the framework can be turned into five separate models, varying in terms of the operating regime for domestic monetary policy.[12] The five alternative operating procedures may be referred to as the portfolio regime, the base regime, the total-reserves regime, the unborrowed-reserves regime, and the funds-rate regime according to whether the main Federal Reserve policy instrument is, respectively, S^{MA}, *B*, *RT*, *RU*, or r^{ff}.

In my schematic framework it is assumed that the Federal Reserve makes decisions about the settings on its instruments (whatever the operating regime) only at periodic meetings. During the interval between meetings, referred to here as the short-run period, the instrument settings are assumed to remain unchanged at the values chosen at the last decision (that is, chosen at "the beginning of the period"). In contrast, it is assumed that the nonpolicy exogenous forces in the framework can change *during* the period. The analysis that follows focuses on the consequences of unexpected nonpolicy disturbances occurring during

12. See Ralph C. Bryant, *Money and Monetary Policy in Interdependent Nations* (Brookings Institution, 1980), chap. 14, for further discussion of the distinction between potential and actual policy instruments and of alternative operating regimes for domestic monetary policy.

the short run, that is, disturbances that have effects *before* the Federal Reserve reconsiders its instrument settings.

Consider the procedures followed by the Federal Reserve at one of its periodic decisions. In principle, the Federal Reserve may be described as implementing policy in several logical steps. It will first specify its objectives and the trade-offs among them (in technical terms, its "loss function" or "welfare criterion"). It will then make projections for each of the nonpolicy exogenous forces in its model of the economy; the best projection for the change in each of these nonpolicy forces might be, but need not be, a value of zero. Finally, it will insert the projections of the nonpolicy exogenous forces into its model and, subject to its loss function, select those values for its instrument settings that, ex ante, have the greatest likelihood of achieving its policy objectives.

I do not believe that the Federal Reserve should use the money stock as an intermediate-target variable in its decisionmaking (see chapter 8). But for the purposes of this appendix, it is immaterial what strategy the Federal Reserve follows. In particular, the reader can imagine that the Federal Reserve seeks a specific target value for the money stock in each short-run period and that no other variable enters into its loss function. In that event, the Federal Reserve would select its instrument settings at the beginning of each period to attain exactly its target value for M (subject to its ex ante projections of the nonpolicy exogenous forces).

The nonpolicy exogenous forces in the schematic framework for which the Federal Reserve must make projections are Flt, Dep^G, u_{RX}, u_{RR}, u_{BR}, u_C, u_D, and Y. Projected changes for these variables are *expected* changes and are thus taken into account when the Federal Reserve determines its instrument settings at the beginning of the period. *Unexpected* changes in these nonpolicy variables—referred to hereafter as disturbances—are the differences between actual changes during the period and the Federal Reserve's projections of the changes. (By definition, $\Delta\tilde{u}_j \equiv \Delta u_j - \Delta\hat{u}_j$ where $\Delta\hat{u}_j$ is the projected change in u_j and $\Delta\tilde{u}_j$ is the unexpected disturbance.)

Portfolio Regime

Consider first the regime in which the Federal Reserve uses S^{MA} as its main policy instrument. Of the five alternative regimes, this one is the least "activist." The Federal Reserve at the beginning of a short-run period chooses a value for its security portfolio and then effectively "sits on its hands." No unexpected change in any of the nonpolicy disturbances gives rise to induced open-market operations. The security portfolio, because set initially at the chosen value, remains constant.

A set of reduced-form equations for the money stock and for four of the other endogenous variables for this portfolio regime is

$$\text{(A-11)}\quad \begin{bmatrix} \Delta M \\ \Delta r^{ff} \\ \Delta RT \\ \Delta RU \\ \Delta B \end{bmatrix} = \frac{1}{\delta_1} \begin{bmatrix} (a_1 + a_2) & -c(a_1 + a_2) \\ 1 & -c \\ ha_2 & -c(ha_2) \\ (ha_2 - c) & ca_1 \\ (ha_2 + a_1) & -c(ha_2 + a_1) \end{bmatrix} \begin{bmatrix} \Delta S^{MA} \\ \Delta r^d \end{bmatrix}$$

$$+ \frac{1}{\delta_1} \begin{bmatrix} (a_1 + a_2) & -(a_1 + a_2) & \delta_1(b_1 + b_2) - (a_1 + a_2)(b_1 + hb_2) \\ 1 & -1 & -(b_1 + hb_2) \\ ha_2 & -ha_2 & -b_1(ha_2) - hb_2(c - a_1) \\ (ha_2 - c) & -(ha_2 - c) & -b_1(ha_2 - c) + hb_2a_1 \\ (ha_2 + a_1) & -(ha_2 + a_1) & -c(b_1 + hb_2) \end{bmatrix} \begin{bmatrix} \Delta Flt \\ \Delta Dep^G \\ \Delta Y \end{bmatrix}$$

$$+ \frac{1}{\delta_1} \begin{bmatrix} \delta_1 - (a_1 + a_2) & \delta_1 - h(a_1 + a_2) & -(a_1 + a_2) & -(a_1 + a_2) & (a_1 + a_2) \\ -1 & -h & -1 & -1 & 1 \\ -ha_2 & -h(c - a_1) & -(c - a_1) & -(c - a_1) & ha_2 \\ -(ha_2 - c) & ha_1 & a_1 & a_1 & -a_1 \\ \delta_1 - (ha_2 + a_1) & -hc & -c & -c & (ha_2 + a_1) \end{bmatrix} \begin{bmatrix} \Delta u_C \\ \Delta u_D \\ \Delta u_{RR} \\ \Delta u_{RX} \\ \Delta u_{BR} \end{bmatrix},$$

where $\delta_1 = ha_2 + a_1 - c < 0$.

Base Regime

If the Federal Reserve decides to use the monetary base as its main instrument, it must stand ready to conduct open-market operations to offset any incipient change in B that would otherwise deflect B from its predetermined value. (By definition, open-market operations are purchases or sales of securities and hence a change in S^{MA}.) In particular, the Federal Reserve must be prepared to offset, automatically and routinely, changes in *Flt*, Dep^G, and *BOR* as they occur.[13] The need to offset these three sources of possible change can be grasped by examining

13. What is presumed is that the Federal Reserve continuously monitors what is happening to B and promptly conducts offsetting sales or purchases of securities to counter any incipient change in B away from the predetermined value set at the beginning of the period.

the following rewritten version of the balance-sheet identity, equation A-1:

$$\text{(A-1a)} \qquad \Delta B \equiv \Delta S^{MA} + (\Delta Flt - \Delta Dep^{G} + \Delta BOR).$$

If the left-hand side of this identity is to stay unchanged at a predetermined value, then any incipient unanticipated changes in the three variables inside the parentheses must be offset by movements in the opposite direction of the security portfolio. Note that in this base regime an unanticipated change in the demand for currency does *not* require an offsetting open-market operation; an unexpected change in Δu_C will alter the composition of the base between *CUR* and *RT* but will not change *B* itself.

The set of reduced-form equations derived from equations A-1 through A-10 under the assumption that the Federal Reserve uses the base regime as its preferred operating procedure is

$$\text{(A-12)} \quad \begin{bmatrix} \Delta M \\ \Delta r^{ff} \\ \Delta RT \\ \Delta RU \\ \Delta S^{MA} \end{bmatrix} = \frac{1}{\delta_2} \begin{bmatrix} (a_1 + a_2) & 0 \\ 1 & 0 \\ ha_2 & 0 \\ (ha_2 - c) & c(\delta_2) \\ \delta_2 - c & c(\delta_2) \end{bmatrix} \begin{bmatrix} \Delta B \\ \Delta r^{d} \end{bmatrix}$$

$$+ \frac{1}{\delta_2} \begin{bmatrix} 0 & 0 & \delta_2(b_1 + b_2) - (b_1 + hb_2)(a_1 + a_2) \\ 0 & 0 & -(b_1 + hb_2) \\ 0 & 0 & h(b_2 a_1 - b_1 a_2) \\ 0 & 0 & -b_1(ha_2 - c) + hb_2(c + a_1) \\ -\delta_2 & \delta_2 & c(b_1 + hb_2) \end{bmatrix} \begin{bmatrix} \Delta Flt \\ \Delta Dep^{G} \\ \Delta Y \end{bmatrix}$$

$$+ \frac{1}{\delta_2} \begin{bmatrix} \delta_2 - (a_1 + a_2) & \delta_2 - h(a_1 + a_2) & -(a_1 + a_2) & -(a_1 + a_2) & 0 \\ -1 & -h & -1 & -1 & 0 \\ -ha_2 & a_1 h & a_1 & a_1 & 0 \\ -(ha_2 - c) & h(c + a_1) & (c + a_1) & (c + a_1) & -\delta_2 \\ c & hc & c & c & -\delta_2 \end{bmatrix} \begin{bmatrix} \Delta u_C \\ \Delta u_D \\ \Delta u_{RR} \\ \Delta u_{RX} \\ \Delta u_{BR} \end{bmatrix}$$

where $\delta_2 = ha_2 + a_1 < 0$.

Total-Reserves Regime

Under an operating regime in which the Federal Reserve selects a predetermined value for RT and holds that value unchanged during the short-run interval between policy decisions, induced open-market operations will be routinely required to offset changes in Flt, Dep^G, BOR, and CUR. If such automatic adjustments in S^{MA} were not made, changes in these four variables would move the instrument RT away from its predetermined value. This point can be easily seen, again, by rearrangement of the balance-sheet identity, equation A-1:

$$\text{(A-1b)} \quad \Delta RT \equiv \Delta S^{MA} + (\Delta Flt - \Delta Dep^G + \Delta BOR - \Delta CUR).$$

The left-hand side of A-1b can be kept unchanged at a predetermined value only if ΔS^{MA} is adjusted up (down) to offset incipient unanticipated declines (increases) in the sum of the four variables in parentheses.

The set of reduced-form equations for the total-reserves regime derived from the analytical framework of equations A-1 through A-10 is

$$\text{(A-13)} \quad \begin{bmatrix} \Delta M \\ \Delta r^{ff} \\ \Delta RU \\ \Delta S^{MA} \\ \Delta B \end{bmatrix} = \frac{1}{\delta_3} \begin{bmatrix} (a_1 + a_2) & 0 \\ 1 & 0 \\ (ha_2 - c) & c(\delta_3) \\ (ha_2 + a_1 - c) & c(\delta_3) \\ (ha_2 + a_1) & 0 \end{bmatrix} \begin{bmatrix} \Delta RT \\ \Delta r^d \end{bmatrix}$$

$$+ \frac{1}{\delta_3} \begin{bmatrix} 0 & 0 & \delta_3(b_1 + b_2) - hb_2(a_1 + a_2) \\ 0 & 0 & -hb_2 \\ 0 & 0 & hb_2c \\ -\delta_3 & \delta_3 & \delta_3 b_1 + hb_2(c - a_1) \\ 0 & 0 & h(b_1a_2 - b_2a_1) \end{bmatrix} \begin{bmatrix} \Delta Flt \\ \Delta Dep^G \\ \Delta Y \end{bmatrix}$$

$$+ \frac{1}{\delta_3} \begin{bmatrix} \delta_3 & \delta_3 - h(a_1 + a_2) & -(a_1 + a_2) & -(a_1 + a_2) & 0 \\ 0 & -h & -1 & -1 & 0 \\ 0 & hc & c & c & -\delta_3 \\ \delta_3 & h(c - a_1) & (c - a_1) & (c - a_1) & -\delta_3 \\ \delta_3 & -h & -1 & -1 & 0 \end{bmatrix} \begin{bmatrix} \Delta u_C \\ \Delta u_D \\ \Delta u_{RR} \\ \Delta u_{RX} \\ \Delta u_{BR} \end{bmatrix},$$

where $\delta_3 = ha_2 < 0$.

Unborrowed-Reserves Regime

Under this regime induced open-market operations are required to offset unanticipated changes in Flt, Dep^G, and CUR but are not required to offset unanticipated changes in BOR:

$$\text{(A-1c)} \qquad \Delta RU \equiv \Delta S^{MA} + (\Delta Flt - \Delta Dep^G - \Delta CUR).$$

When an unanticipated change in borrowings occurs, there is a change in RT and B; the instrument value for RU, however, is left unchanged.

The set of reduced-form equations for this unborrowed-reserves regime is

$$\text{(A-14)} \quad \begin{bmatrix} \Delta M \\ \Delta r^{ff} \\ \Delta RT \\ \Delta S^{MA} \\ \Delta B \end{bmatrix} + \frac{1}{\delta_4} \begin{bmatrix} (a_1 + a_2) & -c(a_1 + a_2) \\ 1 & -c \\ ha_2 & -c(ha_2) \\ \delta_4 + a_1 & -ca_1 \\ ha_2 + a_1 & -c(ha_2 + a_1) \end{bmatrix} \begin{bmatrix} \Delta RU \\ \Delta r^d \end{bmatrix}$$

$$+ \frac{1}{\delta_4} \begin{bmatrix} 0 & 0 & \delta_4(b_1 + b_2) - hb_2(a_1 + a_2) \\ 0 & 0 & -hb_2 \\ 0 & 0 & -hb_2c \\ -\delta_4 & \delta_4 & \delta_4 b_1 - hb_2 a_1 \\ 0 & 0 & \delta_4 b_1 - hb_2(c + a_1) \end{bmatrix} \begin{bmatrix} \Delta Flt \\ \Delta Dep^G \\ \Delta Y \end{bmatrix}$$

$$+ \frac{1}{\delta_4} \begin{bmatrix} \delta_4 & \delta_4 - h(a_1 + a_2) & -(a_1 + a_2) & -(a_1 + a_2) & (a_1 + a_2) \\ 0 & -h & -1 & -1 & 1 \\ 0 & -hc & -c & -c & ha_2 \\ \delta_4 & -a_1 h & -a_1 & -a_1 & a_1 \\ \delta_4 & -h(c + a_1) & -(c + a_1) & -(c + a_1) & ha_2 + a_1 \end{bmatrix} \begin{bmatrix} \Delta u_C \\ \Delta u_D \\ \Delta u_{RR} \\ \Delta u_{RX} \\ \Delta u_{BR} \end{bmatrix},$$

where $\delta_4 = ha_2 - c < 0$.

Funds-Rate Regime

The four operating procedures discussed above are all "quantity regimes" in the sense that the Federal Reserve chooses one or another financial quantity on its balance sheet as its main policy instrument. The last of the regimes considered here is, in contrast, a "price regime": the Federal Reserve chooses for its main instrument the short-term interest rate that is the "price" of immediately available funds in the interbank market, r^{ff}. To keep r^{ff} at a predetermined value, the Federal Reserve must be ready to execute a sufficiently large volume of open-market transactions (increases or decreases in S^{MA}) to offset any incipient change in r^{ff} that would otherwise occur.

If the Federal Reserve chooses this operating regime, then *all* the quantities on its balance sheet become endogenous variables. In effect, the Federal Reserve is able to keep the "price" r^{ff} at a predetermined instrument setting during the interval between policy decisions only by allowing market demands and supplies to determine the "quantity" of funds available.

The set of reduced-form equations for five of the endogenous quantity magnitudes for the funds-rate regime is

$$\text{(A-15)}\quad \begin{bmatrix} \Delta M \\ \Delta RT \\ \Delta RU \\ \Delta S^{MA} \\ \Delta B \end{bmatrix} = \frac{1}{\delta_5} \begin{bmatrix} -(a_1 + a_2) & 0 \\ -ha_2 & 0 \\ -(ha_2 - c) & -c \\ -(ha_2 + a_1 - c) & -c \\ -(ha_2 + a_1) & 0 \end{bmatrix} \begin{bmatrix} \Delta r^{ff} \\ \Delta r^{d} \end{bmatrix}$$

$$+ \frac{1}{\delta_5} \begin{bmatrix} 0 & 0 & -(b_1 + b_2) \\ 0 & 0 & -hb_2 \\ 0 & 0 & -hb_2 \\ 1 & -1 & -(b_1 + hb_2) \\ 0 & 0 & -(b_1 + hb_2) \end{bmatrix} \begin{bmatrix} \Delta Flt \\ \Delta Dep^{G} \\ \Delta Y \end{bmatrix}$$

$$+ \frac{1}{\delta_5} \begin{bmatrix} -1 & -1 & 0 & 0 & 0 \\ 0 & -h & -1 & -1 & 0 \\ 0 & -h & -1 & -1 & 1 \\ -1 & -h & -1 & -1 & 1 \\ -1 & -h & -1 & -1 & 0 \end{bmatrix} \begin{bmatrix} \Delta u_C \\ \Delta u_D \\ \Delta u_{RR} \\ \Delta u_{RX} \\ \Delta u_{BR} \end{bmatrix},$$

where $\delta_5 = -1$.

Table A-4. *Comparison of the Effects of an Unexpected Increase in Float or an Unexpected Reduction in the Government's Deposit Balance under the Five Alternative Operating Regimes*

Endogenous variable affected	*Operating procedure for monetary policy*				
	Portfolio regime	*Base regime*	*Total-reserves regime*	*Unborrowed-reserves regime*	*Funds-rate regime*
M	$\frac{(a_1 + a_2)}{ha_2 + a_1 - c} > 0$	0	0	0	0
r^{ff}	$\frac{1}{ha_2 + a_1 - c} < 0$	0	0	0	**r^{ff} is an exogenous instrument**
S^{MA}	**S^{MA} is an exogenous instrument**	−1	−1	−1	−1

Source: Equations A-11 through A-15. For definitions of the endogenous variables see table 2-1, note a.

Consequences of Nonpolicy Disturbances

Chapters 2 and 3 discuss the effects of the various nonpolicy disturbances under the five alternative operating regimes. The remainder of this appendix presents the analytical results on which that summary is based.

Float and the Government's Deposit Balance

Table A-4 extracts the results from the reduced-form equations A-11 through A-15 that show the consequences under the five operating regimes of an unexpected increase in float (and also an unexpected decrease in the government's deposit balance). Under all regimes except the portfolio regime, changes in *Flt* and Dep^G have no effect on the money stock and the federal funds rate.

Excess Reserves and Required Reserves

For any given operating regime, the consequences of an unexpected change in excess reserves, $\Delta \tilde{u}_{RX}$, and an unexpected change in required reserves, $\Delta \tilde{u}_{RR}$, are identical. Table A-5 provides a comparison of these results for the five operating regimes.

Consider first the effects on the federal funds rate. Under all four quantity regimes, r^{ff} rises. (Under the funds-rate regime, r^{ff} is an instrument and does not change at all from its predetermined setting.) For negative values of the coefficients a_1 and a_2 and positive values of c and h, the following inequalities always hold:

$$0 < \frac{-1}{ha_2 + a_1 - c} < \frac{-1}{ha_2 - c} < \frac{-1}{ha_2},$$

Funds-rate regime	Portfolio regime	Unborrowed-reserves regime	Total-reserves regime

$$0 < \frac{-1}{ha_2 + a_1 - c} < \frac{-1}{ha_2 + a_1} < \frac{-1}{ha_2}.$$

Funds-rate regime	Portfolio regime	Base regime	Total-reserves regime

Table A-5. *Comparison of the Effects of an Unexpected Increase in Excess Reserves (or an Unexpected Increase in Required Reserves) under the Five Alternative Operating Regimes*

	Operating procedure for monetary policy				
Endogenous variable affected	*Portfolio regime*	*Base regime*	*Total-reserves regime*	*Unborrowed-reserves regime*	*Funds-rate regime*
M	$\frac{-(a_1 + a_2)}{ha_2 + a_1 - c} < 0$	$\frac{-(a_1 + a_2)}{ha_2 + a_1} < 0$	$\frac{-(a_1 + a_2)}{ha_2} < 0$	$\frac{-(a_1 + a_2)}{ha_2 - c} < 0$	0
r^{ff}	$\frac{-1}{ha_2 + a_1 - c} > 0$	$\frac{-1}{ha_2 + a_1} > 0$	$\frac{-1}{ha_2} > 0$	$\frac{-1}{ha_2 - c} > 0$	**r^{ff} is an exogenous instrument**
S^{MA}	**S^{MA} is an exogenous instrument**	$\frac{c}{ha_2 + a_1} < 0$	$\frac{c - a_1}{ha_2} < 0$	$\frac{-a_1}{ha_2 - c} < 0$	1

Source: Same as table A-4.

The relative sizes of $|a_1|$ and c—the interest responsiveness of, respectively, nonbanks' currency demand and banks' demand for discount-window borrowing—determine whether r^{ff} rises more or less under the base regime than under the unborrowed-reserves regime. If, as seems probable (see appendix B), *BOR* is more sensitive than *CUR* to interest rates, r^{ff} will rise less under the unborrowed-reserves regime; that is,

$$\underset{\text{Unborrowed-reserves regime}}{\frac{-1}{ha_2 - c}} < \underset{\text{Base regime}}{\frac{-1}{ha_2 + a_1}} \qquad \text{if} \quad c > |a_1|.$$

The consequences for the money stock are analogous to those for r^{ff}. Under the funds-rate regime, M remains undisturbed. Under the four quantity regimes, the money stock declines in response to the rise in interest rates. When discount-window borrowing is more interest-sensitive than currency demand, the sizes of the declines are ranked as follows:

$$\underset{\text{Funds-rate regime}}{0} > \underset{\text{Portfolio regime}}{\frac{-(a_1 + a_2)}{ha_2 + a_1 - c}} > \underset{\text{Base regime}}{\frac{-(a_1 + a_2)}{ha_2 + a_1}} > \underset{\text{Unborrowed-reserves regime}}{\frac{-(a_1 + a_2)}{ha_2 - c}} > \underset{\text{Total-reserves regime}}{\frac{-(a_1 + a_2)}{ha_2}}.$$

For the less likely case in which $|a_1|$ is larger instead of smaller than c, the relative positions of the base regime and the unborrowed-reserves regime in the above ranking are reversed.

Discount-Window Borrowing

Table A-6 presents a comparison of the consequences of an unexpected increase in bank borrowing at the discount window, $\Delta\tilde{u}_{BR}$.

Under three of the five operating procedures—the funds-rate regime, the total-reserves regime, and the base regime—there are no "unplanned" changes in M and r^{ff} due to the unexpected increase in borrowing. Under these regimes, induced open-market operations produce a decline in the Federal Reserve security portfolio that exactly offsets the surprise surge in *BOR*.

Under the unborrowed-reserves regime and the portfolio regime the federal funds rate falls and induces an unplanned increase in the money

Table A-6. *Comparison of the Effects of an Unexpected Increase in Discount-Window Borrowing under the Five Alternative Operating Regimes*

Endogenous variable affected	*Operating procedure for monetary policy*				
	Portfolio regime	*Base regime*	*Total-reserves regime*	*Unborrowed-reserves regime*	*Funds-rate regime*
M	$\frac{(a_1 + a_2)}{ha_2 + a_1 - c} > 0$	0	0	$\frac{(a_1 + a_2)}{ha_2 - c} > 0$	0
r^{ff}	$\frac{1}{ha_2 + a_1 - c} < 0$	0	0	$\frac{1}{ha_2 - c} < 0$	**r^{ff} is an exogenous instrument**
S^{MA}	**S^{MA} is an exogenous instrument**	−1	−1	$\frac{a_1}{ha_2 - c} > 0$	−1

Source: Same as table A-4.

stock. The unplanned changes are larger under the unborrowed-reserves regime than under the portfolio regime for any values of the behavioral coefficients; for example, the effects on the money stock are

$$\underset{\substack{\text{Unborrowed-}\\\text{reserves}\\\text{regime}}}{\frac{(a_1 + a_2)}{ha_2 - c}} > \underset{\substack{\text{Portfolio}\\\text{regime}}}{\frac{(a_1 + a_2)}{ha_2 + a_1 - c}} > 0.$$

Autonomous Deposit Demand

The consequences of an unexpected autonomous increase in deposit demand, $\Delta\tilde{u}_D$, are compared in table A-7. For reasons given in chapter 2, this disturbance is one for which changes in r^{ff} are undesirable. The preferred outcome is for M to increase dollar for dollar with the unexpected change in demand.

The sizes of the interest-rate responses under the five regimes are ranked as follows for the case in which $c > |a_1|$:

$$\underset{\substack{\text{Funds-}\\\text{rate}\\\text{regime}}}{0} < \underset{\substack{\text{Portfolio}\\\text{regime}}}{\frac{-h}{ha_2 + a_1 - c}} < \underset{\substack{\text{Unborrowed-}\\\text{reserves}\\\text{regime}}}{\frac{-h}{ha_2 - c}} < \underset{\substack{\text{Base}\\\text{regime}}}{\frac{-h}{ha_2 + a_1}} < \underset{\substack{\text{Total-}\\\text{reserves}\\\text{regime}}}{\frac{-h}{ha_2}}.$$

The effects on the money stock are derivative from the changes in r^{ff}. Among the four quantity regimes, M rises the most under the portfolio regime. Under the total-reserves regime, M actually contracts.

Autonomous Currency Demand

Table A-8 collects the results for unexpected disturbances to currency demand, $\Delta\tilde{u}_C$.

For the total-reserves, the unborrowed-reserves, and the funds-rate regimes, induced open-market operations supply exactly the incremental amount of currency demanded; no rise in r^{ff} occurs; M rises with the increase in currency.

Under the portfolio and the base regimes, r^{ff} must rise to restore balance in the demand for and supply of immediately available funds. The extent of the rise is sufficiently great under the base regime to induce

Table A-7. *Comparison of the Effects of an Unexpected Autonomous Increase in Deposit Demand under the Five Alternative Operating Regimes*

Endogenous variable affected	Operating procedure for monetary policy				
	Portfolio regime	*Base regime*	*Total-reserves regime*	*Unborrowed-reserves regime*	*Funds-rate regime*
M	$1 - \frac{h(a_1 + a_2)}{ha_2 + a_1 - c} > 0$	$1 - \frac{h(a_1 + a_2)}{ha_2 + a_1} > 0$	$1 - \frac{h(a_1 + a_2)}{ha_2} < 0$	$1 - \frac{h(a_1 + a_2)}{ha_2 - c} > 0$	1
r^{ff}	$\frac{-h}{ha_2 + a_1 - c} > 0$	$\frac{-h}{ha_2 + a_1} > 0$	$\frac{-h}{ha_2} > 0$	$\frac{-h}{ha_2 - c} > 0$	**r^{ff} is an exogenous instrument**
S^{MA}	**S^{MA} is an exogenous instrument**	$\frac{hc}{ha_2 + a_1} < 0$	$\frac{h(c - a_1)}{ha_2} < 0$	$\frac{-a_1 h}{ha_2 - c} < 0$	$h > 0$

Source: Same as table A-4.

Table A-8. *Comparison of the Effects of an Unexpected Autonomous Increase in Currency Demand under the Five Alternative Operating Regimes*

Endogenous variable affected	Operating procedure for monetary policy: Portfolio regime	Base regime	Total-reserves regime	Unborrowed-reserves regime	Funds-rate regime
M	$1 - \frac{(a_1 + a_2)}{ha_2 + a_1 - c} \gtrless 0$	$1 - \frac{(a_1 + a_2)}{ha_2 + a_1} < 0$	1	1	1
r^{ff}	$\frac{-1}{ha_2 + a_1 - c} > 0$	$\frac{-1}{ha_2 + a_1} > 0$	0	0	**r^{ff} is an exogenous instrument**
S^{MA}	**S^{MA} is an exogenous instrument**	$\frac{c}{ha_2 + a_1} < 0$	1	1	1

Source: Same as table A-4.

Table A-9. *Comparison of the Effects of an Unexpected Increase in Nominal Economic Activity under the Five Alternative Operating Regimes*

Endogenous variable affected	*Operating procedure for monetary policy*				
	Portfolio regime	*Base regime*	*Total-reserves regime*	*Unborrowed-reserves regime*	*Funds-rate regime*
M	$(b_1 + b_2) - \frac{(b_1 + hb_2)(a_1 + a_2)}{ha_2 + a_1 - c}$	$(b_1 + b_2) - \frac{(b_1 + hb_2)(a_1 + a_2)}{ha_2 + a_1}$	$(b_1 + b_2) - \frac{hb_2(a_1 + a_2)}{ha_2}$	$(b_1 + b_2) - \frac{hb_2(a_1 + a_2)}{ha_2 - c}$	$(b_1 + b_2) > 0$
r^{ff}	$\frac{-(b_1 + hb_2)}{ha_2 + a_1 - c} > 0$	$\frac{-(b_1 + hb_2)}{ha_2 + a_1} > 0$	$\frac{-hb_2}{ha_2} > 0$	$\frac{-hb_2}{ha_2 - c} > 0$	**r^{ff} is an exogenous instrument**
S^{MA}	**S^{MA} is an exogenous instrument**	$\frac{c(b_1 + hb_2)}{ha_2 + a_1} < 0$	$b_1 + \frac{hb_2(c - a_1)}{ha_2} \lesseqgtr 0$	$b_1 - \frac{hb_2 a_1}{ha_2 - c} \gtreqless 0$	$(b_1 + hb_2) > 0$

Source: Same as table A-4.

a contraction in M. The rise in r^{ff} under the portfolio regime is less than under the base regime; M may either rise or fall, depending on the relative sizes of the interest-response coefficients a_1, a_2, and c.

Unexpected Changes in Aggregate Demand

Disturbances originating in the goods markets or labor markets of the economy are likely to change the nominal value of economic activity. Changes in aggregate demand expected by the Federal Reserve are taken into account when instrument settings are selected at the periodic meetings. Unexpected changes in $Y(\Delta\tilde{Y})$, however, lead to increases or decreases in the demand for deposits and currency.

Ultimate targets of policy such as inflation and output growth will be adversely affected by unexpected disturbances originating outside financial markets. The greater the resistance provided by financial markets to such disturbances, the better the outcome for the economy. For example, when aggregate demand is unexpectedly high, the preferred outcome is for interest rates to rise to help restrain the adverse consequences.

The sizes of interest-rate responses under the alternative operating regimes depend on the income coefficients in the money-demand functions, b_1 and b_2, as well as the interest-rate coefficients a_1, a_2, and c (table A-9). For an increase in aggregate demand, it is always true for the increases in r^{ff} that

$$\underset{\text{Total-reserves regime}}{\frac{-hb_2}{ha_2}} > \underset{\text{Unborrowed-reserves regime}}{\frac{-hb_2}{ha_2 - c}} > \underset{\text{Funds-rate regime}}{0}$$

and

$$\underset{\text{Base regime}}{\frac{-(b_1 + hb_2)}{ha_2 + a_1}} > \underset{\text{Portfolio regime}}{\frac{-(b_1 + hb_2)}{ha_2 + a_1 - c}} > \underset{\text{Funds-rate regime}}{0.}$$

Unless the interest-rate elasticity of currency demand is very small and the income elasticity of currency demand is unusually large, the funds rate is likely to rise more under the total-reserves regime than under the base regime and more under the portfolio regime than under the unborrowed-reserves regime. Other rankings of the interest-rate responses are mathematically possible, though less plausible.[14]

The largest rise in the money stock induced by an unexpected increase in aggregate demand occurs under the funds-rate regime. The dampening of the increase in *M* under the four quantity regimes is proportionate to the rise in r^{ff}. Hence the sizes of the increases in *M* are most plausibly ranked as funds-rate regime > unborrowed-reserves regime > portfolio regime > base regime > total-reserves regime. For plausible values of the coefficients, *M* may even fall under the total-reserves regime.

14. If one uses the mechanically derived estimates in Tinsley, "A Field Manual for Stochastic Money Market Impacts," as a basis for judging the magnitudes of a_1, a_2, c, h, b_1, and b_2, the statement in the text about the most plausible rankings of the alternative regimes is valid.

APPENDIX B

Empirical Equations

THE EMPIRICAL EQUATIONS used to derive figures 4-3, 4-4, 4-6, and 4-8 are explained in this appendix, and some additional information is provided to supplement the discussion in chapter 4.

Deposit Demand

The demand equation for the deposit component of M1 used to simulate the predicted series in figure 4-3 is shown in equation B-1. The equation is taken from the summer 1981 version of the monthly money-market model used by the staff of the Federal Reserve Board.[1] It was estimated for the sample period from January 1971 through December 1979. The variables in the equation are specified as growth rates (the first differences of the natural logarithms of the underlying series) and the constant term was accordingly suppressed during estimation. This version is the "real" rather than the alternate, "nominal" specification of the equation; that is, the dependent variable is (the growth rate of) the nominal value of deposits deflated by a price index, not (the growth rate of) the nominal value of deposits itself.

$$\text{(B-1)} \quad \Delta \ln \left[\frac{D}{P}\right] = \underset{(4.48)}{-0.006DCON} + \sum_{i=0}^{6} a_i \Delta \ln (r^{fp}_{-i}) + \sum_{i=0}^{3} b_i \Delta \ln (r^{t*}_{-i}) + \sum_{i=0}^{5} c_i \Delta \ln \left[\frac{Y_{-i}}{P_{-i}}\right] + \sum_{i=0}^{3} d_i \Delta \ln (P_{-i}) + \underset{(4.05)}{0.363U_{-1}}$$

Adjusted $R^2 = 0.149$; standard error of the regression $= 0.00493$; Durbin-Watson $= 2.11$.

1. See Helen T. Farr, "The Monthly Money Market Model," Federal Reserve Board staff working paper (July 1981), p. 10.

where D = demand deposits plus other checkable deposits (the deposit component of M1) measured in billions of dollars seasonally adjusted, monthly averages of daily data

P = implicit price deflator for personal consumption expenditures, 1972 = 100, from the U.S. national income and product accounts

Y = personal income in current prices, measured in billions of dollars at a seasonally adjusted annual rate, from the U.S. national income and product accounts

r^{fp} = interest rate on thirty-day directly placed finance company paper, percent per year

r^{t*} = interest rate on small time-deposits, constructed in the manner suggested by Fitzgerald, percent per year[2]

$DCON$ = dummy variable equal to 1.0 from April 1974 through March 1977, otherwise equal to 0

U_{-1} = correction term for first-order serial correlation in the residuals of the uncorrected equation (its coefficient being the estimated value of rho).

The lag coefficients in equation B-1 are as follows:

Lag (month)	*Effects of r^{fp} (a_i)*	*Effects of r^{t*} (b_i)*	*Effects of Y/P (c_i)*	*Effects of P (d_i)*
0	−0.022	−0.009	0.143	−0.969
1	−0.022	−0.012	0.180	0.164
2	−0.021	−0.012	0.193	0.566
3	−0.019	−0.008	0.181	0.239
4	−0.016	. . .	0.145	. . .
5	−0.012	. . .	0.085	. . .
6	−0.006	. . .	. . .	. . .
Sum of lag coefficients (*t*-statistics)	−0.119 (−11.4)	−0.041 (−3.52)	0.927 (4.52)	0
Constraints	$\Sigma a_i = -0.16$ ($k = 0.15$)	$\Sigma b_i = -0.05$ ($k = 0.15$)	. . .	$\Sigma d_i = 0$

Equation B-1 was estimated by the Federal Reserve Board staff with restricted least squares (in the case of two variables, with inexact constraints; the values of k are given in parentheses beneath the con-

2. The construction of this interest rate is described in Helen T. Farr, "Derivation of the Fitzgerald Time Deposit Rate Used in the Monthly Money Market Model," Federal Reserve staff working paper (1979).

straints). I was able to estimate an equation roughly similar to B-1 without the restrictions on the coefficients. In that unrestricted regression, however, the sum of the coefficients on the finance-paper interest rate was only −0.038 (for the restricted equation it was −0.119), the sum of the coefficients on the interest rate on small time-deposits was −0.030 (relative to −0.041), the sum of the coefficients on real personal income was 0.777 (rather than 0.927), and the sum of the coefficients on the price variable was −0.326 (the restricted equation forces the sum to 0). Simulation of that equation generated a predicted series qualitatively similar to that obtained from equation B-1. In the unrestricted regression there was no significant autocorrelation of the residuals (the Durbin-Watson statistic was 2.33).

Equation B-1 is subject to many of the same problems that afflict all deposit-demand and money-demand equations for years subsequent to 1973. These problems have been discussed by many economists; see, for example, the analyses by Goldfeld, by Enzler, Johnson, and Paulus, by Tinsley and Garrett, by Porter, Simpson, and Mauskopf, by Simpson and Porter, by Wenninger, Radecki, and Hammond, by members of the staff of the Federal Reserve Board in the 1981 staff study of the new operating procedures, by Hester, and by Lindsey.[3] The dummy variable *DCON* included in equation B-1 is a "rough and ready" way of correcting

3. See Stephen M. Goldfeld, "The Case of the Missing Money," *Brookings Papers on Economic Activity, 3:1976*, pp. 683–730; Jared Enzler, Lewis Johnson, and John Paulus, "Some Problems of Money Demand," *Brookings Papers on Economic Activity, 1:1976*, pp. 13–54; Peter A. Tinsley and Bonnie Garrett with Monica Friar, "The Measurement of Money Demand," Special Studies Paper 133 (Federal Reserve Board, Division of Research and Statistics, 1978); Peter A. Tinsley and Bonnie Garrett with Monica Friar, "An Expose of Disguised Deposits," *Journal of Econometrics*, vol. 15 (1981), pp. 117–37; Richard D. Porter, Thomas D. Simpson, and Eileen Mauskopf, "Financial Innovation and the Monetary Aggregates," *Brookings Papers on Economic Activity, 1:1979*, pp. 213–29; Thomas D. Simpson and Richard D. Porter, "Some Issues Involving the Definition and Interpretation of the Monetary Aggregates," in Federal Reserve Bank of Boston, *Controlling the Monetary Aggregates III*, Conference Series, no. 23 (1980), pp. 161–234; John Wenninger, Lawrence Radecki, and Elizabeth Hammond, "Recent Instability in the Demand for Money," *Federal Reserve Bank of New York Quarterly Review*, vol. 6 (Summer 1981), pp. 1–9; David E. Lindsey and others, "Monetary Control Experience under the New Operating Procedures," in Board of Governors of the Federal Reserve System, *New Monetary Control Procedures*, vol. 2 (The Board, 1981); Donald D. Hester, "Innovations and Monetary Control," *Brookings Papers on Economic Activity, 1:1981*, pp. 141–99; and David E. Lindsey, "Nonborrowed Reserve Targeting and Monetary Control," in Lawrence Meyer, ed., *Improving Money Stock Control: Problems, Solutions, and Consequences* (Federal Reserve Bank of St. Louis, 1982). Similar problems are also discussed by Anthony M. Solomon, "Financial Innovation and Monetary Policy," remarks before the joint luncheon of the American Economic and American Finance Associations, Washington D.C., December 28, 1981.

for the especially large errors that the equation would otherwise produce for the 1974–77 period.[4]

Equation B-1 incorporates a correction term for first-order serial correlation in the residuals of the uncorrected equation. The corrected equation presumably contains less inadequate estimates of the coefficients than those obtained from the uncorrected equation. As can be seen in figure 4-3, however, major changes in the predicted series typically follow major changes in the actual series with a lag of one month. The fact that the autocorrelation correction term carries a significant part of the burden of keeping the predicted series close to the path of actual deposits suggests strongly that the corrected equation is still not an adequate representation of the aggregate behavior underlying deposit demand.

For the purposes of this book I did not try to replicate and simulate a deposit equation containing an interest-rate ratchet variable of the sort proposed by Simpson and Porter and discussed by Lindsey and others.[5] Such an equation would probably have generated a predicted series with somewhat smaller errors in 1979–81 than those plotted in figure 4-3. The errors for 1982, however, could well have been somewhat larger. Use of the Simpson-Porter specification would not overturn the general conclusion that deposit demand has been subject to large shifts not readily attributable to changes in interest rates, prices, and real income.

Currency Demand

The variable explained in the equation underlying figure 4-4, *CUR*, is the nondeposit component of M1—that is, the sum of currency in circulation outside banks plus the outstanding traveler's checks of nonbank issuers. *CUR* is measured in billions of dollars and is seasonally

4. Two recent papers provide some evidence that casts strong doubt on the desirability of adjusting the equation in this rough and ready way. See Peter A. Tinsley, P. A. V. B. Swamy, and Bonnie Garrett, "The Anatomy of Uncertainty in a Money Market Model," unpublished paper presented at the December 1981 ASSC Meetings (December 1981), and P. A. V. B. Swamy, Peter A. Tinsley, and G. R. Moore, "An Autopsy of a Conventional Macroeconomic Relation: The Case of Money Demand," Special Studies Paper 167 (Federal Reserve System, Division of Research and Statistics, April 1982).

5. See Simpson and Porter, "Some Issues Involving the Definition and Interpretation of the Monetary Aggregates"; Lindsey and others, "Monetary Control Experience Under the New Operating Procedures"; and Lindsey, "Nonborrowed Reserve Targeting and Monetary Control."

adjusted; the observations are monthly averages of daily figures. As in equation B-1 of this appendix, the dependent variable in the equation as actually estimated is the growth rate of "real" rather than nominal balances. The other variables in the equation—P, Y, and r^{fp}—are the same series for, respectively, the price deflator for personal consumption expenditures, the nominal value of personal income, and the interest rate on thirty-day finance-company paper used in equation B-1. The sample period for estimation was January 1971 through September 1979. The equation was estimated with the constant term suppressed and without correction for serial correlation in the residuals. Details of the currency equation are shown below.

$$\text{(B-2)} \qquad \Delta \ln \left[\frac{CUR}{P}\right] = \sum_{i=0}^{10} a_i \Delta \ln (r^{fp}_{-i}) + \sum_{i=0}^{9} c_i \Delta \ln \left[\frac{Y_{-i}}{P_{-i}}\right] + \sum_{i=0}^{4} d_i \Delta \ln (P_{-i})$$

Adjusted $R^2 = 0.430$; standard error of the regression $= 0.00207$; Durbin-Watson $= 1.81$.

The lag coefficients in equation B-2 are

Lag (month)	*Effects of r^{fp} (a_i)*	*Effects of Y/P (c_i)*	*Effects of P (d_i)*
0	−0.0043	0.121	−0.501
1	−0.0041	0.110	−0.097
2	−0.0039	0.099	0.155
3	−0.0036	0.088	0.255
4	−0.0033	0.076	0.203
5	−0.0030	0.064	. . .
6	−0.0026	0.052	. . .
7	−0.0021	0.039	. . .
8	−0.0017	0.026	. . .
9	−0.0012	0.013	. . .
10	−0.0006	. . .	. . .
Sum of lag coefficients (standard error)	−0.030 (0.007)	0.688 (0.084)	0.014 (0.051)

Equation B-2 is a variant of the equation for currency plus traveler's checks in the monthly money-market model of the Federal Reserve Board staff.[6] The Board staff variant imposes the restriction that the sum

6. Farr, "The Monthly Money Market Model," p. 6.

of coefficients on the current and lagged terms of the price variable equal zero. I did not use a restricted least squares technique when replicating the equation; the unrestricted coefficients, however, match those in the Board staff variant fairly closely.

Both the deposit and the currency equations above exhibit a sizable negative elasticity of demand with respect to interest rates. As shown by the recent work of Swamy and Tinsley and their colleagues, the estimated interest-rate coefficients in deposit and currency equations tend to be a major source of uncertainty if one abandons the traditional but questionable assumption that all uncertainty is confined to the intercept terms of fixed coefficient equations. The interest-rate coefficients in equations B-1 and B-2 should therefore be taken with several grains of salt.[7]

Excess Reserves

The equation for excess reserves underlying figure 4-6 is shown below as equation B-3. It is a variant of the equations reported in papers by Tinsley and others.[8]

$$\text{(B-3)}\quad \ln(RX) = \underset{(0.299)}{-1.855} - [\ln(rff)]\left[\underset{(0.051)}{0.402} - \underset{(0.171)}{1.960}\left(\frac{CAR}{0.02RR}\right)\right] + \underset{(0.051)}{0.103}(\ln SCMB) + \underset{(0.007)}{0.187}U_{-1} + \textit{seasonal effects}$$

Adjusted $R^2 = 0.643$; standard error of the regression $= 0.120$; Durbin-Watson $= 2.09$,

7. See Swamy, Tinsley, and Moore, "An Autopsy of a Conventional Macroeconomic Relation: The Case of Money Demand," and Tinsley, Swamy, and Garrett, "The Anatomy of Uncertainty in a Money Market Model." Another relevant discussion is Thomas F. Cooley and Stephen F. LeRoy, "Identification and Estimation of Money Demand," *American Economic Review*, vol. 71 (December 1981), pp. 825–44.

8. Memorandum, S. H. Axilrod to Board of Governors of the Federal Reserve System, "Contemporaneous Reserve Requirements: A Review of Operational and Monetary Control Considerations," including memorandum, Peter A. Tinsley and others to the Board, "Estimated Monetary Policy Consequences of Reserve Accounting Procedures," September 14, 1981, pp. 30–36; Tinsley, Swamy, and Garrett, "The Anatomy of Uncertainty in a Money Market Model"; and "Policy Robustness: Specification and Simulation of a Monthly Money Market Model," *Journal of Money, Credit and Banking*, vol. 14 (November 1982), pt. 2, pp. 829–56. The figures in parentheses here and in equations in the remainder of this appendix are standard errors of the estimated coefficients.

where

RX = quantity of excess reserves, measured in billions of dollars

rff = federal funds rate, percent per year

CAR = amount of reserves carried over by member banks under carry-over privileges, billions of dollars

RR = required reserves of member banks, billions of dollars

$SCMB$ = a "scale" measure of the size of member banks, defined as reservable deposits (demand, other checkable, time, and savings) less required reserves, billions of dollars

U_{-1} = a correction term for first-order serial correlation in the residuals of the uncorrected equation.

All variables are not seasonally adjusted and are monthly averages of daily data. The equation adjusts for seasonality by including dummy variables for eleven of the twelve months, where the dummy for a particular month is equal to 1 in that month and 0 otherwise.[9] The sample period for estimation is October 1968 through September 1979.

Equation B-3 uses a variable for reserve carry-over, scaled by 2 percent of required reserves (the maximum conceivable amount of carry-over), to modify the estimate of the negative response of excess reserves to the federal funds rate. As explained by Tinsley and his colleagues, an increase in carry-over reduces the effective elasticity of excess reserves with respect to the funds rate.[10]

In my effort to replicate the equations reported by Tinsley and his colleagues, I was unable to estimate as high an elasticity of excess reserves to the scale variable representing the size of member banks' investable funds. Their papers report an elasticity of about 0.3 (or impose that constraint on the equation). Equation B-3 has an estimate of only 0.1.

The discussion in chapter 4 calls attention to the fact that equation B-3 consistently underpredicts excess reserves for the entire period from October 1979 through June 1982. This underprediction may be attributable, at least in part, to adjustments in the banks' behavior in response to the October 1979 change in the Federal Reserve's operating proce-

9. A majority of the seasonal dummies are statistically significant at the 0.05 level.

10. See memorandum, Peter A. Tinsley and others to Board of Governors of the Federal Reserve System, "Estimated Monetary Policy Consequences of Reserve Accounting Procedures," pp. 30–36. I am grateful to Paul Spindt for providing me with data for the amounts of reserve carry-over. The data I used differ somewhat from the carry-over data used by Tinsley and his colleagues; this fact may help to explain the differences between my estimates of the equation and theirs.

dures. Whatever the explanation for the errors, the equation is not a satisfactory one for predicting the demand for excess reserves after 1979.[11]

I am not aware of other efforts to estimate an excess-reserves equation that improve upon the recent results of Tinsley and his colleagues. The conclusion drawn from figure 4-6—that unexpected variations in excess reserves can be a disruptive influence on interest rates and the money stock in the short run—would therefore probably be strengthened by using some other form of excess-reserves equation to generate the predicted series.

Borrowing at the Discount Window

The borrowing by banks at the discount window is negatively related to the spread between the federal funds rate and the discount rate.[12] Substantial uncertainty nonetheless exists about the best specification to use in estimating this relation. The complex interaction of the administrative procedures for borrowing at the various Federal Reserve district banks and the accounting procedures for reserve requirements (see chapter 6) are not easily captured in any single equation for borrowing, or indeed in any set of equations explaining borrowings and excess reserves in a model of bank behavior.

In exploring alternative equations to use in generating a predicted series for borrowing, I tried several possibilities but eventually settled on a variant of the specification recently proposed by Peter Tinsley and

11. The predicted series in figure 4-6 contains a correction factor for autocorrelation in the residuals; see equation B-3. If a predicted series is generated without the correction for autocorrelation, the extent of the underprediction in 1980–82 is even greater.

12. See, for example, Peter Keir, "Impact of Discount Policy Procedures on the Effectiveness of Reserve Targeting," with an appendix by Dana Johnson and others; and Fred Levin and Paul Meek, "Implementing the New Procedures: The View from the Trading Desk," in Board of Governors of the Federal Reserve System, *New Monetary Control Procedures* (The Board, 1981), vol. 1; Perry D. Quick, "Federal Reserve Discount Window Procedures and Monetary Control: Two Modest Proposals," unpublished manuscript (1981); Farr, "The Monthly Money Market Model"; Vefa Tarhan and Paul A. Spindt, "Bank Earning Asset Behavior and Causality Between Reserves and Money: Lagged versus Contemporaneous Accounting," *Journal of Monetary Economics* (forthcoming); and D. H. Resler and others, "Detecting and Estimating Changing Economic Relationships: The Case of Discount Window Borrowings," Special Studies Paper 165 (Federal Reserve System, August 1982).

his colleagues at the Federal Reserve Board.[13] This specification uses a hyperbolic-tangent transformation of an adjusted measure of the spread between the funds rate and the discount rate. More precisely, where the spread, *SPR*, is defined as $SPR = r^{ff} - r^{d}$, positive values of *SPR* are multiplied by 0.5 and negative values are multiplied by 2.0 to generate an adjusted spread series, *SADJ*; the hyperbolic-tangent transformation,

$$\tanh(x) = \frac{e^{x} - e^{-x}}{e^{x} + e^{-x}},$$

is then used to obtain the variable tanh (*SADJ*) to be used as a regressor in the equation for borrowing.

The equations for borrowing in the papers by Tinsley and colleagues use another variable that behaves similarly to an interest rate, a measure of deposit risk due to Tinsley and Garrett. This variable, *DRISK*, is defined as

$$DRISK = \frac{1}{\Sigma\, Dep}[(r^{max})(DDep) + (r^{max} - r^{sav})(SAVDep + OCDep) + (r^{max} - r^{stim})(STIMDep) + (r^{max} - r^{ltim})(LTIMDep)],$$

where *DDep*, *SAVDep*, *OCDep*, *STIMDep*, and *LTIMDep* are, respectively, demand deposits, savings deposits, other checkable deposits, small time deposits, and large time deposits at member banks; ΣDep is the sum of all five types of deposits; r^{sav}, r^{stim}, and r^{ltim} are, respectively, the interest rates paid by banks on savings deposits, small time deposits, and large time deposits (CDs); and r^{max} is an interest-rate series equal in each month to the maximum value of r^{sav}, r^{stim}, r^{ltim}, or the three-month Treasury bill rate. *DRISK* is a measure of the opportunity yields forgone by deposit owners, where higher opportunity yields are assumed to increase the risk to the banks of deposit withdrawals.

The remaining independent variable in the equations for borrowing specified by Tinsley and colleagues is a scale measure of the size of banks, *SCMB*, defined earlier in the discussion of equation B-3.

Two estimates of an equation for borrowing covering the sample period from October 1968 through September 1979 are shown below.

13. See Tinsley and others, "Estimated Monetary Policy Consequences of Reserve Accounting Procedures," pp. 36–43, and the modified form of the specification in Tinsley, Swamy, and Garrett, "The Anatomy of Uncertainty in a Money Market Model" and in Peter A. Tinsley and others, "Policy Robustness: Specification and Simulation of a Monthly Money Market Model," *Journal of Money, Credit and Banking*, vol. 14 (November 1982), pt. 2, pp. 829–56.

Equation B-4 does not have, whereas B-5 does, a correction term for first-order serial correlation in the residuals (U_{-1}). The coefficients on the explanatory variables in the two equations, in particular the coefficient on tanh (*SADJ*), are nontrivially different.

$$\text{(B-4)} \qquad \ln(BOR) = \underset{(1.02)}{-3.225} + \underset{(0.11)}{1.497} \tanh(SADJ) + \underset{(0.20)}{0.361} \ln(DRISK) + \underset{(0.17)}{0.312} \ln(SCMB)$$

Adjusted $R^2 = 0.799$; standard error of the regression $= 0.5057$; Durbin-Watson $= 0.57$.

(B-5)

$$\ln(BOR) = \underset{(2.59)}{-3.103} + \underset{(0.15)}{1.252} \tanh(SADJ) + \underset{(0.30)}{0.407} \ln(DRISK) + \underset{(0.43)}{0.287} \ln(SCMB) + \underset{(0.003)}{0.749}(U_{-1})$$

Adjusted $R^2 = 0.465$; standard error of the regression $= 0.3498$; Durbin-Watson $= 2.17$.

The dependent variable in B-4 and B-5 is the natural logarithm of a series for borrowing, *BOR*, that excludes emergency credit to the Franklin National Bank in 1974 and to the First Pennsylvania Bank in 1980. The data for *BOR* used in the projections for 1981 and 1982 also exclude the new category of "extended credit" borrowing inaugurated in August 1981. In its computations of intermeeting reserve paths for the FOMC and in its weekly statistical releases, the Federal Reserve treats this extended-credit borrowing as though it were part of unborrowed reserves rather than discount-window borrowing.[14] That treatment and the underlying differences in procedures at the discount window argue for not including extended-credit borrowing in an equation representing the bulk of regular borrowing. *BOR* is measured in billions of dollars not seasonally adjusted; the observations are monthly averages of daily figures.

In an equation for the same sample period and corrected for first-order serial correlation, Tinsley and colleagues obtain a lower estimated value of rho (between 0.4 and 0.5) and somewhat higher values for the estimated coefficients (above 1.6 for the tanh (*SADJ*) variable, above 0.4 for the deposit-risk variable, and above 0.8 for the variable measuring

14. Extended-credit borrowing is made available to depository institutions facing liquidity problems that are not promptly reversible, and the borrowing therefore has a longer maturity than seasonal and normal adjustment borrowing.

bank scale). I have not yet been able to account for these discrepancies; they may be attributable to minor differences in the data sets.

Predicted series and the associated errors from equations B-4 and B-5 are shown in, respectively, figures B-1 and B-2. Those figures cover the entire period from February 1975 through June 1982. (Figure B-1 is identical to figure 4-8, except that the latter covers the shorter period from October 1979 through June 1982.)

Ordinarily an equation with serial correlation in the residuals as severe as that in equation B-4 would be thought inferior to a corrected equation. That judgment may be correct here, too. The regression standard error for this equation is significantly larger than that for B-5. From figure B-2, however, one can observe that the correction for autocorrelation in equation B-5 plays a critical but worrisome role. The predicted series from that equation follows along fairly closely after the actual series, but much of the time with a one-month lag, thus systematically missing many of the peaks and troughs in borrowing as they occur. The smaller errors in figure B-2 relative to those in figure B-1 are due primarily to the mechanical correction in equation B-5 for three-fourths of the equation's failure in each previous month. A strong suspicion exists, therefore, that the corrected equation is not at all satisfactory and that it, too, like equation B-4, may not have generated reliable estimates of the "true" coefficients.

Because the surcharge on discount-window borrowing imposed in March–April 1980 and between November 1980 and November 1981 occurred after the estimation sample period of October 1968 through September 1979, equations B-4 and B-5 make no allowance for that institutional change in discount-window procedures.[15] The large negative residuals for those months in figure B-1 (which are not mechanically dampened by the autocorrelation correction) can probably be explained, in part, by the failure of the tanh (*SADJ*) variable—or of some other aspect of the specification—to reflect the effects of the surcharge.

Given the failure of the equation specification to take account of the surcharge and given the suspiciously important role of the correction for autocorrelation in equation B-5, a case can be made that equation B-4

15. The surcharge was 300 basis points during April 1980. During June, July, and August of 1981 it was 400 basis points, after having been 300 basis points between December 1980 and May 1981.

Figure B-1. *Discount-Window Borrowing: Actual, Predicted, and Prediction Error from Equation without Correction for Autocorrelation, January 1975 to June 1982*[a]

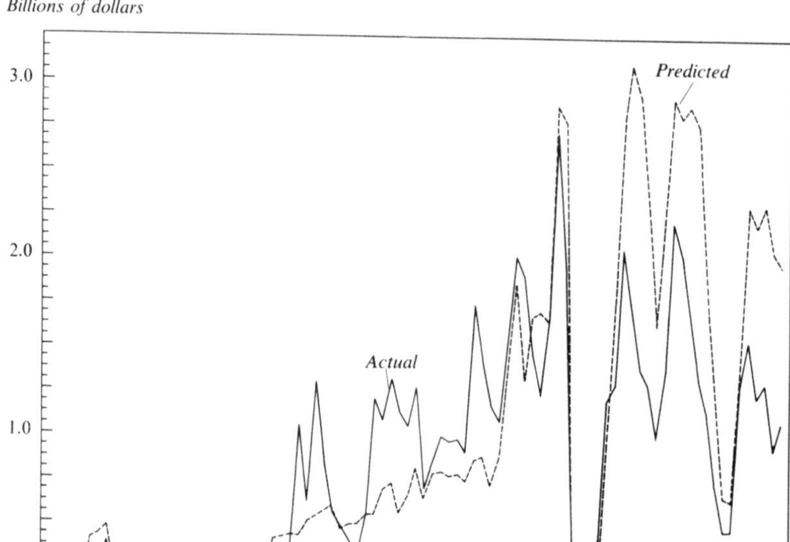

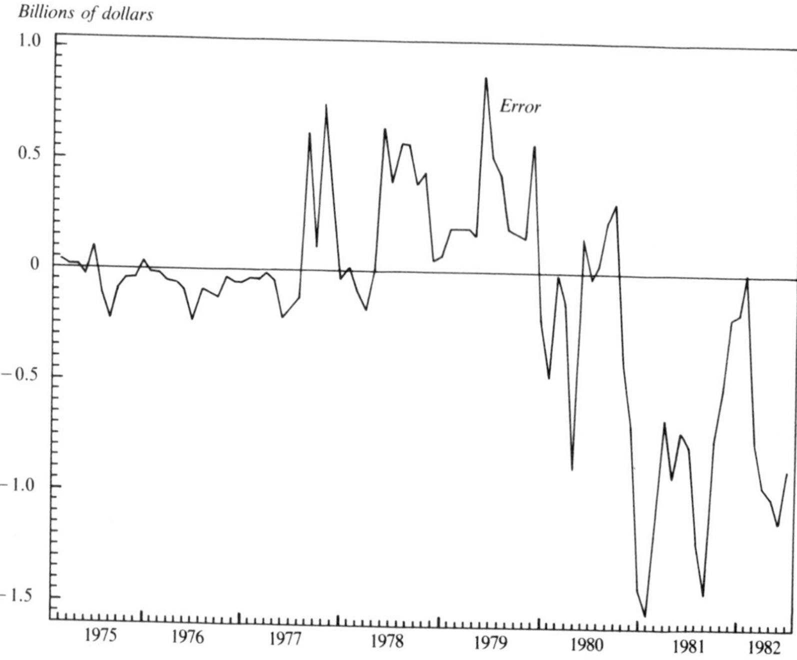

Source: Board of Governors of the Federal Reserve System.

a. Equation B-4 was used to generate the predicted series. Data are monthly averages of daily data, not seasonally adjusted.

Figure B-2. *Discount-Window Borrowing: Actual, Predicted, and Prediction Error from Equation with Correction for Autocorrelation, January 1975 to June 1982*[a]

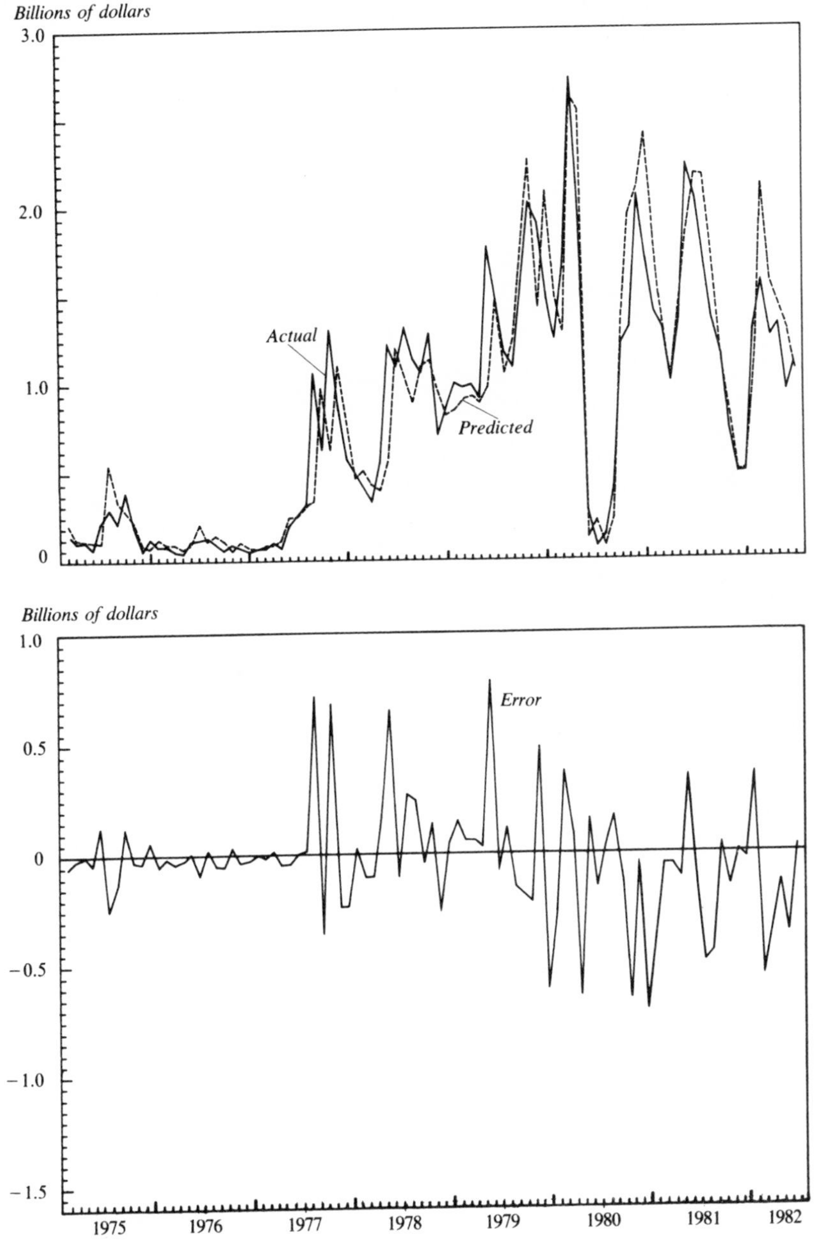

Billions of dollars

3.0

2.0

Actual

1.0

Predicted

0

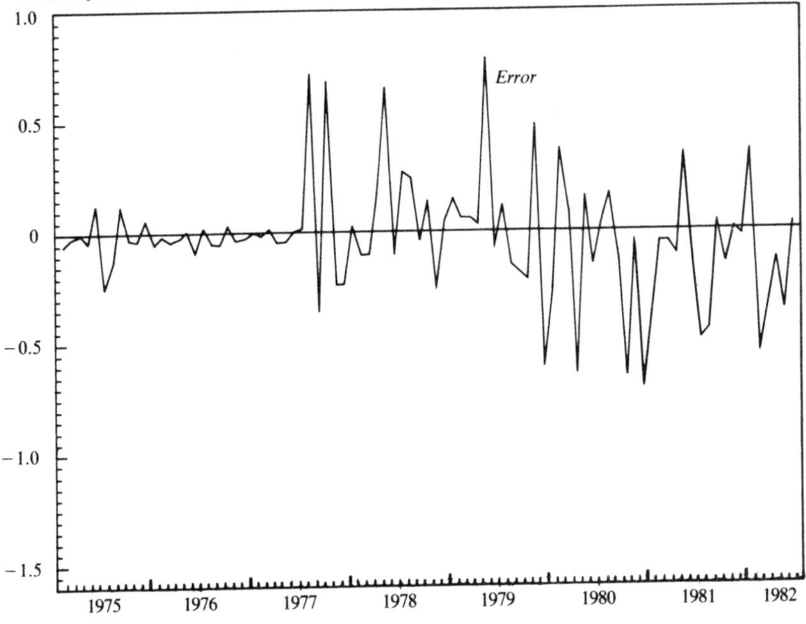

Source: Board of Governors of the Federal Reserve System.

a. Equation B-5 was used to generate the predicted series. Data are monthly averages of daily data, not seasonally adjusted.

may be the less unreliable of the two. That at any rate was my rationale for using equation B-4 in constructing figure 4-8 in chapter 4.

It is not possible to make any simple adjustment in these two equations to reflect the surcharge because of the complexities of its administration. For example, only the advances made to large banks were subject to the surcharge, and only then if those banks were frequent borrowers. Merely to add the amount of the surcharge to the discount rate before calculating the *tanh(SADJ)* variable, therefore, would overcorrect for the effects of the surcharge.[16]

Neither equation is satisfactory. Again, however, the conclusion stated in chapter 4 is not likely to be altered qualitatively by the use of a different equation: discount-window borrowing is subject to substantial variations that are not entirely predictable and that can have significant effects on short-term interest rates and the money stock.

16. I also calculated and plotted the analogues of figures B-1 and B-2 using data for the spread between the federal funds rate and the discount rate "corrected" for the surcharge in this mechanical manner. As surmised, the predicted series for borrowing in those calculations falls well *below* actual borrowing during the period the surcharge was in effect.

Index